GESTURES
OF
GENIUS:
WOMEN,
DANCE,
AND THE
BODY

GESTURES
OF
GENIUS:
WOMEN,
DANCE,
AND THE
BODY

Rachel Vigier

THE MERCURY PRESS

The publisher gratefully acknowledges the financial assistance of the Canada Council and the Ontario Arts Council, as well as that of the Government of Ontario through the Ontario Publishing Centre.
The interview with Crowsfeet Dance Collective was first published in *FUSE*.

Edited by Beverley Daurio
Cover design by Gordon Robertson
Cover photograph: Detail of a photograph by Sam Kanga
Author photograph by Lori Stevens
Composition and page design by TASK

Printed and bound in Canada by Metropole Litho
Printed on acid-free paper
First Edition
1 2 3 4 5 98 97 96 95 94

Canadian Cataloguing in Publication Data

Vigier, Rachel, 1955-
Gestures of genius : women, dance, and the body
ISBN 1-55128-012-4
1. Women dancers.
I. Title
GV1799.4.V55 1994   792.8'082   C94-932112-5

Represented in Canada by the Literary Press Group
Distributed by General Distribution Services

The Mercury Press
137 Birmingham Street
Stratford, Ontario
Canada   N5A 2T1

FOR MY GRANDMOTHER
WHO LOVED TO DANCE
HÉLÈNE DESHAYES BRICK

ACKNOWLEDGEMENTS

While writing this book, I met many generous and gifted people who shared their knowledge and experience of dance with me. I would like to thank my dance teachers in Toronto and New York, the women I first danced with in the basement of the Palmerston Library in Toronto, and the people I studied and performed with in New York. As well I would like to thank the dancers who were interviewed for this book.

I especially would like to thank my long-time friends Carol Brooks and Kathy Zinger. I benefited from Carol and Kathy's insight and from their search for a more generous language of the body.

M. Nourbese Philip provided years of encouragement during the work involved in writing and publishing a first book.

Women's Workshop, a non-profit educational centre for women in London, Ontario, provided me with much needed financial assistance during my first year in New York. The Explorations Program of the Canada Council also provided financial assistance during the final stages of this work.

Finally, I would like to thank my family for their support and understanding.

Marlene

CONTENTS

THE
LARGER
GESTURE

To inhabit one's body is cause for celebration.
Simone de Beauvoir

Like millions of women, I want to write my body into struggle, because something tells me— and it is not my male science— that a great part of history, never thought out or written by us, has been embedded in the memory of the female body.
Madelaine Gagnon

the female body as psychic and ideological key
arteries which lead to pre-patriarchal junctures
Carolee Schneemann

1. THE TRUTH OF THE BODY

The idea for a book on women and dance first took shape several years ago when I decided to go to New York City to study dance professionally. My decision was not motivated by a desire for a career in concert performance; I was primarily interested in what dance could tell me about ways of knowing that included women and the body. Although I could not have said so then, I was looking to *inhabit* my body.

At the time I made my decision to study dance, I was teaching at a university where the emphasis was on a more abstract learning process. Coming from this environment, I looked forward to being in an environment that valued learning with the body and studying in a field where women have been visible and important, historically.

I was also terrified. I did not fit the typical image of a dance student; I had never studied dance full-time. Till then, I had danced only weekly with a group of women who met in the basement theatre of a public library in Toronto. Not one of us would have dared to call herself a dancer, yet week after week we met to create dances by and for ourselves. Our classes always followed the same pattern. They began with a series of warm-up exercises, to strengthen and stretch our muscles, followed by technical exercises based on patterns of motion and rhythm, and ended with a group improvisation done to music. This group improvisation was always the most satisfying part of the class, an opportunity for each of us to find our movements and gestures within a group. It was our chance to move as women away from judgemental eyes and to know our bodies apart from sexual pressures, concerns of appearance, and expectations of work and family. In a sense, these classes involved consciousness raising at the level of the body, and this was encouraged by our teacher, Doris Mehegan, a dancer and feminist with a strong love of women and the body.

In coming to New York I had intended to follow through on a kind of truth of the body which had been surfacing in me, intellectually and physically, as I looked for a deeper listening of the body. Yet going back over journal entries written during my first year, I find in them a guarded quality, as if I could not permit myself to listen to and trust my body.

Entry from my journal, November 1, 1984
There is much to learn from the body, and not just dance either.
The physicality of our selves is basic to everything we do, yet it is
one of the most neglected aspects of our upbringing and
education, which often serve to trap the reflexes and cauterize the
instincts. Bringing those back to life is, as I'm finding out, an
excruciating process, physically and psychically.

November 8, 1984
Briefly I felt my whole body thinking— a moment of vibration
or alertness, not just in the head but in the legs, the torso, the
arms. A sense of radiating outward from inner movement. A
glimmer that blood, muscle, and bone are knowledgeable and
sentient: consciousness in the curves of muscles, the rushing of
blood, the exchange of fluids and air. Cellular knowledge...

January 10, 1985
In some ways the approach to the body is very male: analyze,
analyze, analyze, and apply the laws. Pull in, push in, lift up— the
desired image is definitely male, androgynous at best, but never
female with curves and roundness, which are considered
"appropriate only for the Middle Eastern belly dancer," our
teacher tells us. This is such a contrast to the way Rina Singha
spoke of her training in Indian dance in the video *Women in Asian
Dance*. "We worked on two pieces, four hours a day for six
months, repeating them over and over again, sometimes with
slight variations and recitation of the rhythmic patterns. In this
way the piece and its timing became a part of our body." She
then demonstrated one of her practice pieces: it could not have
been more than five minutes in all. How I long to train in this
way, slowly repeating what we need to know from the inside.
Our training is done much too quickly, and we are not allowed
the time to really sense the place of movement in the body.

January 23, 1985
The deeper I go into women and dance the more I recognize
myself, get glimpses of what has been lost but is still alive in my
instincts and in the living layers of my body. Yesterday I was
reading about Kabuki theatre, where women are prohibited from
formal participation despite the fact that they created the Kabuki
dance form. Predictably, this form was taken away from them by

men, and they were outlawed from their own creation. Yet a seed of their sensibility remains in the integrity of the form, the wholeness of the dances, which do not fall into abstraction. Here in the *geste* I had a moment of recognition, a tugging in my body saying, *Yes*, we passed here, as I remembered what has fallen into silence, can no longer be said but is still entrusted to the body.

April 23, 1985
More and more I am seeing/sensing how deeply we as women internalize the fact that our bodies are not our own, how deeply the colonization goes. What do we need to free ourselves from the inside? What are the conditions for the freedom of the body? It is as if we have to recompose our most basic posture to find the point or source of all other possibilities.

Those first journal entries, so guarded and wary, neglect the body and the ways we as women have been terrorized out of our bodies. It has taken me a long time to confront the physical madness we live as women, and this knowledge has not come to me through professional dance training. That I did not learn this in the studio is partly due to my own confusion and fear, and partly to deeply embedded habits of making appropriately feminine and approved gestures and movements. But it is also due to the presence of sex role definitions in dance and to the evolution of Western dance as muscular activity, technical behaviour, and visual splash, all of which neglect the deeper powers of the body.

In *Madness and Civilization*, Michel Foucault introduces the idea of physical truth and physical madness. Borrowing a definition of physical truth from the *Encyclopédie*, he writes that,

"Physical truth consists in the accurate relation of our sensations with physical objects"; there will be a form of madness determined by the impossibility of acceding to this form of truth...

Later, he goes on to say that physical madness includes illusions, hallucinations, and perceptual disorders which live in the minds of the insane. Foucault's idea of truth and madness operating at a physical level recognizes the role of the body in determining knowledge and power, though the places occupied by truth and madness must be reversed when speaking of women.

As women, our bodies have no truth in patriarchy other than the legal fictions constructed for us and replicated in abstract and concrete ways. Yet, as we have learned more about women's history and the truth of our lives, we have gained access to a physical truth that goes against patriarchy's legalized fictions. The truth is within our bodies, while the madness— the hallucinations and illusions— belongs to patriarchy's distorted images of women that have nothing to do with our physical truth and everything to do with maintaining control over our bodies. A great part of the physical madness we know originates from the images that surround us and from our culture's denial of the power of our bodies, even in its obsessive and isolating attention to this part of our selves.

In the essay "Professions for Women," Virginia Woolf introduces the Angel in the House who takes over Woolf's pen and encourages the writer to lie and go against herself. The Angel in the House is not interested in women's truth, nor, by virtue of her disembodied form, is she particularly interested in the truth of the body. To survive as a writer with a mind of her own, Woolf determines that she must kill the Angel in the House. Significantly, she relates this murder to a failure to tell the truth about the body. She writes:

These then were two very genuine experiences of my own. These were two of the adventures of my professional life. The first— killing the Angel in the House— I think I solved. She died. But the second, telling the truth about my own experiences as a body, I do not think I solved.

Having destroyed the incorporeal phantom and committed herself to truth, Woolf falls from an angelic pose into the body of a woman. We can only guess at what truths she failed to tell from this troubled embodiment and why she judged herself so harshly, though Woolf herself hints that she failed in telling the passions of a woman's body. What is clear is that Woolf struggled with the truth held in the body and identified it with the making of language.

Since Virginia Woolf wrote these words, women have been telling truths about the body which might have helped Woolf write about the truths which eluded her. The act of writing the body in sex, art, and politics has given us a more detailed understanding of how patriarchy inscribes structures of power and modifies the involvement of human relations at the level of the body. More importantly, it means that women are generating visions of sensitivity and imagination from a once colonized land. Women's gestures in dance have a particularly meaningful place in this work.

Mary Wigman, the German dancer and choreographer— who, in 1914, created a solo piece called the *Witch Dance*, based on women's desire for life— described dance as a balance of "physical movement, spiritual agility, and mental versatility." To her student Hanya Holm, who became one of the pioneers of modern dance in the United States, dance is a "way of thinking." In their practice of dance, Wigman and Holm went to the body as a trusted source of knowledge. By this act, these women, in their art, reversed patriarchy's fundamental opposition to the body and created a form of expression and communication that transforms our most basic sense of self. For Wigman and Holm, the individual is understood as an interconnected organism instead of as a series of conflicting dualities, and the body itself is the foundation of knowledge.

During my first year of study I had the privilege of attending a weekly class with Hanya Holm, who was then in her early nineties. Hanya encouraged us to examine and question every statement she made. "There are no dumb questions," she reminded us week after week. One day, toward the end of the year, I approached her about the relation between the mind and the body. "My mind doesn't know what to do with itself when I listen to my body," I said.

"Do not let your mind dominate your body," she replied. "The mind is there to clarify what the body will do. Trust the body."

In this straightforward statement, this wise old woman reversed for me the whole nightmare of patriarchy visited on women and redrew the relation between the mind and the body. Hanya's simple statement raises issues about creativity, intelligence, power, and the role of the body in the transformation of culture. And, it empowers the individual in her body, where through sexual and reproductive violence women have lived the most destructive aspects of patriarchy. Thinking through the body and providing a historical record of ways in which this has been done is, I believe, one of the most significant contributions dance can make to feminism. The second is related to the creation and impact of images.

In Western culture, women are surrounded by images of the female body that represent male desire and power. The body of women reproduced by advertisers, artists, and pornographers alike mirrors masculinity and is not meant to represent the desires or inner visions of women. By contrast, dance provides us with images that exist for women. This is particularly true of those images preserved from cultures and times where patriarchy had not yet stamped its value on the female body and restricted its meaning under a controlling male gaze.

In going through pictorial histories of dance, I encountered a continuous stream of images where strength, pleasure, and knowledge meet as one in the female form. For the first time, I understood in a visceral way how patriarchal images occupy our inner space, fragmenting and diminishing the power to know and represent an authentic female self. And also for the first time, looking at these representations of women fully immersed in the moment and place measured in their bodies, I felt the power of inviting the body back into itself.

2. WOMEN'S DANCES

All dance began as a sacred activity which allowed humans to reflect on the mysteries of the natural world and the embodiment of these mysterious forces in divine figures. Gestures of invocation and appeasement were directed toward this world, full of magical properties that existed beyond the human will. For women, the role of mother was a central manifestation of these divine and otherworldly forces and was reflected upon in their dancing. The fertility of the body and of the earth, which provided sustenance for the human community, were represented in early dances by women, and the productive and reproductive work of women served as the basis of expression in dance, preserving and communicating gestures necessary for the survival of the community. Apart from their symbolic meaning, the dances in themselves embody the physical unity and affinity of women, who concerned themselves with the survival of their community, together raising children and gathering food.

Records of women's dances date back to the earliest images of humans in the figures of pregnant fertility goddesses found throughout Europe and the Mediterranean. From surviving figurines and cave paintings, we can see that the first recorded human gestures refer simply and directly to women's life-giving powers— the left hand resting on the belly just below the navel, the hands cupping the breasts, or calmly resting on the sex— while the whole body is full and ripe, radiating abundance, sure of its significance in the human and divine order.

The "Venus of Laussel," a limestone relief figure carved in a rock shelter in Laussel, Dordogne, in the south of France, is a good example of the ritualized gestures used to evoke women's life-giving powers. Dating from 25,000-20,000 B.C.E., this figure shows a pregnant woman with her left hand holding her belly while in her raised right hand she holds a curved horn carved with thirteen incisions. Some of these early pregnant goddesses were found in Old European settlements near ovens, in areas of grain preparation, and under the floors of dwellings, indicating that the magic touching of the belly was a necessary gesture for the fruitful accomplishment of food preparation and other household activities. A rock painting from 10,000 B.C.E. found in a cave in Cogul, Spain, shows that these magical properties were extended beyond human activities into the workings of the animal and natural worlds. This painting pictures nine women dancing around a pregnant animal and articulates the affinity between women's power to give birth and the fertility of animals.

Birth gestures appear again much later and in a different form among the Minoan goddesses of Crete, from about 1400-1100 B.C.E. In these figurines, surrounded by fruits and birds or crowned with sacred horns, goddesses stand with upraised arms, palms turned outward in a gesture of fertility and blessing. The snake shrine from 1400-1100 B.C.E. unearthed at Gournia, Crete, which belonged to the snake and childbirth goddess, Eileithyia, also contains a female figure with arms upraised. A more vigorous representation of this gesture is found in a ring seal from Minoan Crete (1600 B.C.E.), in which four female figures with upraised arms perform a dance ritual to invoke the great goddess. In other figurines from this period the serpent as symbol of life and regeneration is entwined around the upraised arms. The undulating movement of the snake was associated with the labouring movement of childbirth and became part of women's dance rituals, as shown by a group of four dancers from Palaikastro, Crete (ca. 1400 B.C.E.), who handle snakes as they perform a circle dance.

In Egypt, records from the eighteenth dynasty (1580-1350 B.C.E.) give evidence of assemblies of women performing ceremonial dances for the purpose of "opening the mother's breasts," a ritual meant to encourage the fertility of women and the earth. This ritual involved dancing in honour of the goddess Hathor, who manifested herself in a variety of forms, most often in the shape of a cow, as the face of the sky, and in the form of the sycamore tree which was thought to be her living body. Hathor, considered to be a goddess of fertility and renewal, was celebrated in dance by gods and goddesses as well as by mortal women. The goddess Satis declared that:

For Her, the gods make music
For Her, the goddesses dance

The sistrum, a rattle-like musical instrument whose sound symbol-ized Hathor, was believed to awaken and stimulate fertility and accom-panied dances performed in Hathor's honour.

The gestures of power and fertility recorded in these early images and ceremonies have been transmitted to us in a vital form through the ancient art of belly dancing. Though popular perception places this dance in a cabaret setting where women perform for the pleasure of male customers, the dance is, in fact, a birth dance originally performed by and for women, a tradition which persists in parts of the Middle East. Belly dancing is made up of movements that emphasize women's sexual and procreative powers and is found in women's dances in different parts of the world. Shaking and rotating the hips, breast shimmies, and belly undulations that mimic the birth movements of labouring women are all part of the dance, and each of these movements relates to the early images of women which emphasized women's breasts, hips, and bellies.

In her colourful and well-documented study on the history of belly dancing, *Belly Dancing: The Serpent and the Sphinx*, Wendy Buonaventura traces the history of belly dancing from these prehistoric images of women. Originally, the dance was an evocation to the great goddess, giver of life, and it is as old as life itself.

> It was used in religious rites, as sympathetic magic to ensure the continuation of the human race and the fertility of the earth. Its sexual movements imitated the process of creation and the mysterious transmission of life through the act of giving birth.

Birth and fertility dances survive to this day in folk traditions all over the world. The ritual of "dancing the baby into the world" still exists in parts of the Middle East and is based on ancient belly dancing movements. Farab Firdoz, a dancer from Saudi Arabia, describes how the labouring woman is surrounded by her tribeswomen, who circle around her, undulating their bellies in sympathy with her body's movements.

In Africa, among the pygmies of Gabon, the first dance takes place in the body of a woman where the embryo tumbles and wriggles in the womb of its mother. From the child's dance in her body the mother intuits the time of delivery, and while she is labouring to give birth the whole community takes up the child's dance outside the mother's hut. When the mother has delivered the child she binds the infant to her and joins in the dance which honours her power to give new life. Using dance to call out the child from its mother's womb is also part of Native American tradition. A Fox woman describes the dance performed by a midwife to assist her during a difficult birth:

> She began singing. She started to go out singing and went around the little wicki-up singing. When she danced by where I was, she knocked on the side. "Come out if you are a boy," she would say. And she would sing again. When she danced by she would again knock on the side. "Come out if you are a girl," she would say again. After she sang four times in a circle she entered the wicki-up. "Now it will be born." Lo, sure enough, a little boy was born.

In Romania, women from a mountain tribe meet once a year to perform a cradle dance that gives thanks for the survival of their newborn children through the harsh winter. Rocking their children, they sing the following melody:

> When my mother was rocking me
> She was singing of longing
> She was singing of longing and I cried
> I've been caught by longing...
> I know I've carried it
> Since my mother sang

And in Africa, the ceremony of the soothing of the mothers by the Gelede society involves dancing as a means of channelling women's fertile energy to benefit the community.

Women's power to bring forth new life was naturally linked to the earth's powers of seasonal regeneration and was equally celebrated in dance ceremonies. In Native American traditions, women are responsible for harvest and thanksgiving dance ceremonies. Among the Iroquois, women are identified with crop fertility and they manage the summer food festivals which involve dance, music, and singing.

On the planted field I walked:
Throughout the fields I went:
Fair fields of corn I saw there:...
I have thanked the sustainers of life.

Usually the women accompany themselves with song and music; however, during some of the women's dances men are called upon as singers. Before the men begin to sing, they consecrate their song to the women by saying, "We do this for our mothers." In the Basket dance, performed by women of the Southwest tribes, women move in long lines, imitating the gestures of grinding corn as they dance in a slow shuffling gait so as not to lose contact with the earth. The women of the Tusayan in New Mexico hold a ten day religious festival called *La-la-konta* which involves games, music, and dancing. The festival is meant to induce the germination of seeds, and during the festival, the women perform a dance to spring. On the second day of the Creek harvesting rite, called the Green Corn dance, the women hold a Ribbon dance. The women wear ribbons streaming from headbands and knives to show that they are willing to prepare food. With their children, the women dance in front of the men to receive their thanks and praise for their part in the harvest.

In Mexico, girls perform a kind of maypole fertility dance, in which the girls twist ribbons in colourful patterns as they dance in a circular motion around a pole. The practice of calling on young girls to summon the earth's powers of growth is present also in European cultures. In eastern Europe, young girls were once called upon to dance over flax fields in the spring to promote the growth of crops. Curt Sachs, in *World History of the Dance,* describes a rain dance known throughout the Balkans, among the southern Slavs, the Bulgarians, the Romanians, the Aromuns, and the Greeks. In this dance, done during times of drought, young girls dance from house to house. In the centre of the circle a young girl, naked except for the grass, leaves, and flowers that decorate her body, dances. As the group moves from house to house, the housewives pour water over the whirling dancer in the centre of the circle.

In Asia, vegetation dances were also performed by goddesses and passed on to mortal women. The goddess Amano-Uzume of Japan performed a type of vegetation dance to call back Amaterasu, the Japanese goddess of the sun and fields. Amaterasu, insulted by her brother's rude behaviour, had withdrawn into a cave and deprived the earth of her light. As the earth became dark and sterile the deities decided to send Amano-Uzume to dance in front of the cave in which Amaterasu had shut herself. Amano-Uzume dressed herself in creeping plants and bamboo leaves and performed a stamping dance on an overturned tub just outside the cave until the sun goddess became curious and peeked out of her cave. As soon as the sun goddess stepped from the cave the deities blocked the cave entrance and she was obliged to return to the world, enticed from her hiding place by the goddess' dance. This fertility dance is believed to be the origin of all Japanese dance, and survived in the ancient shamanistic dances of the *sarume* priestesses in Japan.

Women's strong association with birth and fertility also identifies them with death and regeneration. Marija Gimbutas remarks that "caves and tombs are interchangeable with womb... symbolism," and she devotes a section of her stunning book *The Language of the Goddess* to this aspect of the goddess. Early goddess figurines found in cemeteries or excavated from tombs represent a variation of the original fertility gesture in which one hand touches the belly. In these funerary figurines, both hands are folded across the belly and the body itself is rigidly held and sharply defined, in contrast to the generous and corpulent features of the birth goddesses. Made of bone, ivory, or reindeer antler, they have been found in caves in Dordogne, France, and in Siberia, with the oldest dating from 16,000 B.C.E. Marble figures, ca. 3500-2500 B.C.E., found in Cycladic and Cretan graves, depict the same posture and body type.

In Bulgaria, cave paintings from 4500-4000 B.C.E. show lines of women dancing with one or both hands held to the head in another traditional gesture of death and regeneration. Gimbutas interprets these images as ritual dances performed as part of funeral rites or to invoke the regeneration of the earth. A tradition among the Baronga of the South Pacific takes up this theme. The oldest woman in a Baronga chief's family is called upon to perform a dance three months after the chief's death. She dances a womb dance which imitates movements of sexuality and childbirth to deliver his soul to the other world. And among the Shasta, the Karok, and the Yurok of California, it was sufficient to dance around a woman to start dreaming of the dead.

As a result of women's procreative powers, the female body has been perceived as a doorway which allows access to spiritual and psychic dimensions not normally visible. This power accounts for women's overwhelming presence in shamanistic rites, which involve trance dances that lead the shaman into the spiritual world. From this world, the shaman brings messages to and from the deities and communicates with ancestors for the purposes of divination and healing.

In Japan, shamanism is practised almost exclusively by women, who dance themselves into a trance to enter the world of the dead. During their trance, the shamans draw the dead back to earth and become the "mouth of the dead." If the trance is done for the purpose of divination or to consult with deities about the proper medicines to administer during an illness the shaman becomes the "mouth of the gods." Shamans, many of whom are blind, are trained for a period of three to seven years under the tutelage of an older shaman, who initiates them into the proper rituals. The training period culminates in a ceremony of marriage to a deity, sealed by ecstatic dancing. At the climax of the ceremony, the young girl drops exhausted to the ground and re-emerges from her trance dance symbolically reborn as a full-fledged shaman.

These ancient shamanistic rituals survived in the dances of the *miko* or temple attendants associated with orthodox Shinto temples in Japan. The dances of the *miko* are called *kagura* or *miko-mai*. The women wear long white robes or red skirts and hold bells in their hands as they dance in a group in long, slow strides on the temple's dance floor. The circling movements of the dancers and the noise of the bells is meant to chase away demons. In the west of Japan, the *miko* add a purification rite to the *kagura*. Using bamboo shoots as wands, they sprinkle holy water as they dance by the faithful.

In China, women also made up the largest number of practitioners of shamanism. Most often, they were possessed by the spirits of the dead, which they invited into themselves by dancing in circles until they induced a state of trance. Dance was the preferred means of simulating the magical flight of the spirits from their world into the world of mortals. In order to properly receive the spirit into her body, the shaman purified herself with perfumed water, clothed herself in a ritual costume, and made offerings. Her dance and songs staged the voyage made by the spirits and the moment in which she dropped exhausted to the ground became the moment in which the spirit entered her. During these states, shamans spoke with the voices of the dead and demonstrated extraordinary powers. They could make themselves invisible to others, cut themselves without bleeding, swallow swords and fire, and cause objects to move and dance around them.

A cycle of nine hymns composed in the fourth century B.C.E. by the poet K'iu Yuan survives from the province of Tch'ou. Each of these hymns concerns a divinity which shamans called down to earth by singing and dancing. The last hymn is not dedicated to any particular divinity. It relates to eternity and to the eternal return of the seasons, as danced by groups of young girls holding flowers. The girls danced themselves to the point of exhaustion, and before stopping, transmitted their flowers to the next dancer, who continued to call on the eternal power of the spirits by taking up the dance of her companions.

> The rite is done! Bang on the drums!
> They dance in turns— pass on the flower
> Beautiful young maidens dance— and circle in time.
> Orchids in springtime— chrysanthemums by fall:
> May it be so— forever and ever!

The practice of using young girls as trance mediums occurs also in Bali. According to the Balinese, the trances of the *sanghyang dedari* are provoked by celestial nymphs. One of these nymphs descends from her heavenly position and enters the body of a young girl, evoking in her mortal counterpart an extraordinary ability to dance. Without any training, these young girls perform intricate movements usually performed by *Legong* dancers who study for a period of six months to a year to master the technique. In general, the young girls dance in pairs with their eyes shut in a trance-like state. In some villages, the girls enter these trances only during the harvest season. One source mentions that there was an increase in these dances during the movement for independence early in the twentieth century. Once the girls enter puberty they no longer function as mediums for the celestial nymphs and cease to dance.

In the Middle East, the *zar* ceremony, a dance ritual of exorcism, is used to cure spiritually sick women. The *zar* was introduced in Egypt from the Sudan by Nubian concubines who kept the dance tradition intact in Egyptian harems. The word *zar* means "visited," implying that an evil spirit has visited the body of the afflicted woman. The *zar* is attended by a company of long-haired musicians wearing red dresses. Instruments for a *zar* include mostly percussion instruments such as drums, tambourines, brass vessels, and the *nay* or Egyptian flute. The musicians, usually Sudanese or Ethiopian in origin, are sometimes accompanied by a female singer. During the ceremony, the musicians play a series of rhythms, fifteen in number, to entice the evil spirit from the body of the afflicted woman. The spirit in her responds with vigorous whirling and shaking movements until the patient drops to the floor from exhaustion, having danced the spirit out and freed herself from its evil influence. During this ceremony, which may last for several days, the dancer is attended by her female friends and relatives who may join her in the dance.

A similar rite takes place in Korea, where women make up ninety-five per cent of the practising shamans with an equal percentage of their clients also women. In the ceremonies, a part of the ritual called the *Mugan Kori* invites all those present to participate in the ecstatic movements. The movements are simple— mostly turning, jumping, and hopping to get closer to the divinities and spirits in the sky.

Women have also danced to celebrate the passage from girlhood to womanhood. Among the Aboriginal Australian tribes of the Daly River the name of the ceremony is *Pidjuwakart*. On the occasion of her first menstruation, the young girl is taken by her mother to a hut in the bush away from the camp, where she remains during her entire period. At the end of her period, the women in the village dance in her honour. On the morning of the initiation ceremony itself, the initiate gets up to dance and afterwards is thrown into a waterhole by her companions. The dancing continues throughout the day until late afternoon, when the women and girls dance in a long snake line back to the camp. Men are not allowed to witness this ceremony.

In the islands of the South Pacific, the older women perform a dance called the *Hamath* during the puberty ceremony for girls. In Nauru, older women also performed a sensual and free dance during the puberty ceremony of the daughters of respected landowners. Early missionaries disapproved of this display of female sexuality and the dance has since disappeared.

Among the Moussey of Africa the initiation rites for girls end in vigorous dancing involving energetic hip movements. As part of their initiation costumes, the young girls wear bead masks which veil their faces, and belts of iron bells which echo the rhythms of the drums. The

Gbaya, Banda, and Nybaka, who all practice excision, also incorporate dance into the ritual ceremony which marks this passage into woman-hood. The initiates live in groups outside the village while their wounds heal. At the end of the period of seclusion, they engage in vigorous dancing to show that they have successfully gone through the ordeal and that the excision has "given them strength."

During her first menstruation, the Native American California girl danced for ten nights without stopping in a forward and backward movement. No matter how tired she became, the girl had to continue the dance and show to her community her newly acquired strength as a woman.

In the Apache puberty rites for girls, the initiate becomes White Painted Woman or Mother Earth as she dances out her new relationship with the universe. Her initiation dress is dyed yellow, the colour of pollen and fertility, and is decorated with fringes and symbols to represent sunbeams and the forces of the universe she is invoking. Long before the initiate wears the dress, an old woman sings over it. This ritual dance is an occasion for the entire tribe to celebrate Mother Earth and her acceptance of the blessings women bring to earth.

3. MATERNAL CONSCIOUSNESS

Dance is an art in which women have been and are strong, physically as well as psychically. However, dance also functions within patriarchy, which has fixed the female body within specific meanings determined by men's productive and reproductive needs. In so many areas of women's cultural history we have had to begin by questioning the absence of a historical record and rediscovering lost works. With dance we need to begin by finding ways to distinguish the cultural record women have collectively written on the female body from the patri-archal identity forced on the female body. This work is made more difficult by the absence of the body in language and thought and by the codification of the female body as a sign of male power and desire.

In a letter to her feminist aunt, the Danish writer, Isak Dinesen, comments on the place of the woman dancer in patriarchal society and the reason for her existence:

In my opinion, "manliness" is a human concept; "womanliness" as a rule signifies those qualities in a woman or that aspect of her personality that is pleasing to men, or that they had need of. Men had no particular need for or pleasure from, and therefore no reason to encourage women painters, sculptors, or composers— but they did have for dancers, actresses, singers...

The need for dancers as perceived by Dinesen is a sexual need which excludes all other aspects of the female body, and it is a reflection of patriarchy's related need to control the maternal body. It has taken me a long time to make explicit this connection between dance and the maternal body, an example, I think, of how deeply we have been turned against the maternal body by patriarchy's controlling laws and images. Yet it is evident that as the female body is turned away from the full significance of the maternal to become a sexualized sign of male pleasure and power, the movements of the female dancer are also sexualized into the kind of display observed by Dinesen. This objectification interrupts the development of dance as a spiritual and philosophical expression of the body central to women's culture, and it interrupts an order of knowledge based on the maternal body.

In the dances created by women, the maternal body appears in its widest possible sense, as an expression of a culture formed around the life-giving experiences of the body. When I say that dance is about maternal consciousness I do not mean to imply that all dance refers to motherhood or that mothers alone can dance. What I mean is that dance is about and from the body, and going to the body as the material and structure of knowledge brings to the surface a maternal consciousness which also developed through the care of the body.

As child-bearers and primary caretakers of the young, women's daily life initially revolved around securing and maintaining the life of the body. Archaeological and historical evidence suggests that cooking, grain and animal domestication, ceramics, weaving, medicine, language, and architecture— all activities which ensured the survival of the human community through time— were initiated and developed by groups of women working together to maintain the body they created. According to Evelyn Reed, the Marxist feminist anthropologist whose work in the history of social forms traces the evolution of human society from matrilineal to patrilineal forms:

> It was the female of the species who had the care and responsibility of feeding, tending, and protecting the young. However, as Marx and Engels have demonstrated, all societies both past and present are founded upon labour. So... it was not simply the capacity of women to give birth that played the decisive role, for all females gave birth. What was decisive for the human species was the fact that maternity led to labour— it was in the fusion of maternity and labour that the first human social system was founded. It was women who became the chief producers: the workers and farmers, the leaders in scientific, intellectual, and cultural life.

During most of human history the power to give and maintain life fuelled the transformative core of culture and shaped systems of social relations. This happened as women's capacity to give birth and to nourish their newborn children developed into highly sophisticated cultural innovations which evolved in relation to human need.

The primary need for nourishment and shelter, first satisfied by the mother, evolved into a complex set of activities which significantly affected the evolution of human culture. However, until feminist researchers entered the fields of archaeology and anthropology it was assumed that men's role as hunters dominated human evolution. Now, even the most conservative reading of archaeological evidence supports the importance of women's participation in the survival of prehistoric groups, particularly with regard to their food gathering activities.

As foragers and gatherers, women provided the chief food supply of their group and were responsible for a series of discoveries usually attributed to men. In foraging for food such as edible plants, berries, nuts, roots, and tubers, women observed and studied plant cycles and seasonal changes. They later incorporated this knowledge into agricultural techniques which marked a major change in the life of prehistoric groups. They also became adept at discriminating between poisonous and edible plants and so eventually discovered the healing properties of certain herbs. The invention of containers for carrying and storing food, tools for digging tubers, cutting stalks, and breaking open shells also probably originated with women who applied themselves to solving the problems presented by their foraging activities. As primary caretakers of the young, women's daily lives involved a more stable and sedentary existence than their male counterparts'. And it is probable that as a result, women became the inventors of pottery, weaving, architecture, and cooking—domestic sciences which are the precursors of present technologies and sciences. In all of these activities one thing is clear: the intent and products of women's innovations favoured generation and reflected a deep commitment to the life of the body, while the mother and her spectacular ability to create new life operated as the central metaphor and fact of culture.

As metaphor and fact, the maternal role carried over into systems of social structure which mirrored the living web of relations created and traced through the female body. The theories of matrilineal descent, first proposed by Robert Briffault, J.J. Bachofen, Friedrich Engels and later by feminist scholars such as Evelyn Reed, Marija Gimbutas, and Elise Boulding, show that the first laws of lineage and inheritance were determined through maternal blood ties and followed organic patterns of bloodlines laid down through the female body.

The power to give and maintain life, as well as women's vivid role in exercising this power, were also central themes of ancient religious ritual. In Old Europe, the Mediterranean, and the Near East, the female body is the oldest and most prevalent image of the divine. Artifacts, figurines, and shrines unearthed at major Paleolithic and Neolithic excavation sites show that women's bodies defined the substance of the sacred. The relation between humans and the universe was observed in rituals for a great goddess who appears in three simultaneous aspects: as the life-giving mother, as the death-wielding killer, and as the seed of regeneration.

Marija Gimbutas, who collected the images and symbols of the great goddess, characterizes the signs of the goddess in this way. They are, she says, "constantly moving as a serpent, spiral, or whirl." The motion of these images is representative of the life energy manifest in the body and the natural world of plants, animals, and cosmic phenomena as observed by our ancestors. This motion was naturally expressed in rhythmic gestures and dance rituals which directly engaged the body in the celebration of the life force manifest in the divine female and magnified in the experience of nature. Moon or circle dances mirrored astral cycles of the moon, stars, and planets; birth dances ensured the successful passage of new life from the womb to the larger human community; fertility dances stimulated the growth of the human, animal, and vegetative worlds; labyrinthic dances secured the transformative energy of death; and ecstatic dances such as the serpent dances performed by Cretan priestesses maintained direct contact between humans and the unseen spiritual world. All of these dances were performed by women in imitation of the great goddess, who in turn exemplified and revered the bodily and spiritual identity of the human female.

The ritualized essence of the female body permeated the practical and spiritual imaginations of early human groups. All together, the remnants of their cultures affirm the body as a powerful resource and show a deep-seated belief in the body's fecundity, mixed with curiosity and awe about what the body could and would generate. Though productive and creative activities closely followed the rhythms of the body, creative endeavours were not tyrannized or limited by the exigencies of nature and bodily necessity. Instead, the creative and practical products from these cultures exude a "calm knowledge" (to quote Michel Foucault) of the earth's resources, while the body itself served as model and impetus for technologies and rituals which enhanced the health and material being of the whole community.

RE-THINKING
THE
BODY

A free spirit can exist only in a freed body.
Isadora Duncan

1. POLITICIZING THE BODY

Patriarchy politicizes the body with the aim of asserting male supremacy in human relations. To this end, this culture supports and projects
an understanding of the body which is profoundly contrary to earlier
matrilineal societies' demonstrated sense of the body as a powerful
resource. In patriarchy, the body and creative potential of the father is
privileged over the body and creative potential of the mother. This
shift away from the maternal is evident in the struggle between
matrilineal societies prevalent in Greece during the Bronze Age and
the emerging patriarchal order of the Classical Age. The writings of
classical Greek philosophers and dramatists set forth the developing
principles of a fledgling patriarchal order which positioned the male
body as the directing force of religious and social structures, introducing a use and value of the body predicated on strict control of the female
body, the annihilation of matrilineal culture, and the institution of
severe laws against the body.

> ... bodies politic have always been designed for permanence and their
> laws always understood as limitations imposed upon movement...

Though general, this statement by political theorist Hannah Arendt is applicable to the body politic codified in Greek laws of the classical Hellenic age. The features of the body politic identified by Arendt— permanence and limitation of movement— are initially instituted in the individual body of the citizen of the state. This body is perceived as the first and weakest link in the chain of being between the state— personified in the public body politic— and the individual person of the private body politic.

In its natural state, the body is inclined neither toward permanence nor limited movement. The matrilineal world had responded to this organic fact by developing concepts and technologies that accommo- dated the ever-changing transformations of the body. Social structures followed biological patterns of bloodlines established through the mother and religious rituals evolved from the ever-changing patterns of life, while everyday life was devoted to activities meant to sustain the life of the body and the community. In contrast, the patriarchal Greek world refused the life of the body as a resource and organizing principle, concentrating instead on the establishment of a state body politic which legislated the physical body and turned the power of the body toward the maintenance of the abstract state.

The body's natural condition and exigencies presented a problem for the Greeks which they solved by collapsing the activities of the body into the concept of necessity. The fact of necessity was hidden in the private sphere of the household, where the work of caring for the body was done by women and slaves. Sarah B. Pomeroy, in her work on women in classical antiquity, *Goddesses, Whores, Wives, and Slaves*, describes the daily life of Athenian women isolated in the household. Women of all classes, she writes, worked indoors or around the house, preparing food, fabricating clothing, caring for the young, bathing and grooming men, and attending to the sick. Mostly they remained at home in quarters that Pomeroy describes as dark, squalid, and unsanitary. The sexes had separate living quarters and women occupied the most remote rooms away from the street and public areas of the house. A woman could not buy or sell land, she could not vote, nor could she hold public office. An Athenian woman was so removed from public life she could not even make her own purchases in the market-place.

In this first manifestation of democracy, women were not free. Their close association to the body was seen as a reason to confine them to the private realm and to exclude them from the public life of their community. Participation in the public realm and direction of affairs of state were reserved for male citizens who were freed from the necessities of the body by women and slaves. Women and slaves worked in the household; the male citizen was then free to take his place in the body politic where he could exercise his humanity among other men. Thus the body and women's activities, which had till then defined social, spiritual, and communal values, were abstracted and hidden in the realm of necessity where they were given a lesser social value and subjugated to the activities of men, whose freedom was built on a violation of the body, slaves, and women.

The body of women presented a particular problem to the Greeks, as did the everyday and ritualized activities associated with it. Consequently, much of their philosophical and political activities concerned the regulation of the body with a view to establishing a political body capable of carrying over the wealth and ideology of property owning citizens through generations. Here, the reproductive act itself presented a major obstacle. Mary O'Brien's pioneer study of political theory and the social relations of reproduction, *The Politics of Reproduction*, demonstrates how the uncertainty of paternity in the reproductive act fuelled political activity throughout the centuries, beginning with the Greeks. The central theme of this political activity is control of the female body to ensure men the knowledge of paternity denied them in the actual act of reproduction.

The Greek state provided the certainty which the body failed to contribute to the male condition, through institutionalized isolation of women in the household and through marriage laws which gave an individual man control over a woman's body and the production of children. The confinement of women to the household is a clear demonstration of the "limitation of movement" imposed by the body politic; its sole purpose was to ensure the production of legitimate children who could inherit the father's property. Apparently, it was not enough to confine women to the household and to ensure that they remained there by isolating them economically and politically. The Greeks also felt it necessary to completely remove the creative impulse from the female body. In the *Oresteia,* the playwright Aeschylus dramatizes the destruction of matrilineal kinship ties and has the goddess Athena judge that:

> The mother is no parent of that which is called her child, but only nurse of the new-planted seed that grows. The parent is he who mounts.

With this judgement, women lost their economic and political power and their sexual, spiritual, and creative freedom; their bodies were fragmented to serve the needs of the new political man. Demosthenes, a lawmaker of the fourth century B.C.E., sums up the condition of women in democracy:

> We have mistresses for our enjoyment, concubines to serve our person and wives for the bearing of legitimate offspring.

Philosophically, the body was stripped of the spiritual and social values it had known in the pre-Hellenic, matrilineal world. It was seen under the bare light of pleasure and pain, leaving the Greeks with the job of developing a system of laws and education strong enough to harness the elemental energies of the body for the good of the state. "Education," says Plato in *The Laws,* "... consists in correctly trained pleasures and pains," and in curing the body of its ills— the desire for food, drink, and sex. In *The Laws,* education is identified completely with mastery of the art of dance. The educated man is one who has properly mastered this art while the uneducated man is one who is without dance. Education of the body through dance is of primary importance for proper living and this education must begin in early childhood with the correct ordering of the body's elemental energies. Controlled dance turns the body's posture, its every gesture and action, toward the good of the city-state, shaping the body into a manifestation of the values of the state in the individual.

Plato considered certain rhythms or forms of dancing as correct for the Greek citizen, while others, he thought, encouraged disorderliness in the individual and hence disorderliness in the city-state. In his construction of a utopian society, he advocates the establishment of an office of guardians charged with choosing the proper songs and dances for the city-state. These songs and dances become laws in their own right as they replicate and reinforce the values of the city-state:

> ... this is to be the dogma about it: Let no one voice anything or make any dance movement contrary to the public and sacred songs, or the whole choral exercise of the young, any more than he would go against any other "laws."

Plato identifies two kinds of dances: the war-like, which he calls "The Pyrrhic," and the more moderate "Peaceful" or "Harmony" done in prosperous, tranquil times. The Pyrrhic was actually used as a form of military preparation for Athenian boys and consisted

> in imitating, on the one hand, movements that evade all kinds of blows and missiles— by dodging, giving way completely, jumping up, humble crouching— and then again striving to imitate the opposites to these, aggressive postures involved in striking with missiles— arrows and javelins— and with all sorts of blows

while the Peaceful consisted of noble, well-measured steps. These war-like dances and their peaceful counterparts were considered to be the most political of dances, while the ecstatic dances or rhythms celebrated during certain purification and mystery rites were judged "unpolitical." Identified with the cult of Dionysus, these unpolitical dances refer to women's rituals which were opposed by Greek statesmen.

Traditionally, women were the most prominent members of the Dionysian cult which celebrated the vegetative god Dionysus. This cult was Eastern in origin and may have come to mainland Greece from the Minoans and Myceneans, or, it may have been reintroduced to Greece from northern Thrace or eastern Phrygia after the collapse of the Mycenean civilization. It is related to the cult of the great goddess, and retained in its gestures and props many of the characteristics of earlier matrilineal dances. Vases depict the Maenads or Bacchantes, alone or in groups, handling snakes in a manner similar to the snake-handling rituals of priestesses in Crete. Some of the Maenads are playing flutes or hand drums, and others carry torches or staffs known as *thyrsi*; often their heads are thrown back in gestures of ecstasy. According to classical dance scholar Lillian Lawler, the dances were often performed at night on mountainsides, and were characterized by an orgiastic quality in which the women achieved a state of *enthousiasmos* or "the state of having the god within one." As reminders of women's goddess heritage and of their inner spiritual and sacred nature, as opportunities for women to meet in groups, and as possible occasions for women to freely exercise their sexuality, these dances were in conflict with the emerging state of patriarchy which wanted its women isolated in the household and subject to the individual male citizen.

In the play *The Bacchae*, the Greek dramatist Euripides identifies the danger the Dionysian cult presented to the Greek city-state. Pentheus, king of Thebes, describes the coming of Dionysus to his city:

... something very strange is happening in this town.
They tell me our womenfolk have left their homes—
in ecstasy, if you please—

go gadding to the mountains, the shady mountains,
dancing honour on this brash new god:
this— this Dionysus they've got hold of.
In the middle of each coterie of god-possessed
stands a bowl of wine— brimming.
Afterwards, they go sneaking off one by one
to various nooks
to lie down— with *men*;
giving out they're priestesses,
inspired, of course!

Tiresias, an old blind seer who is preparing himself to join the celebrations, tries to persuade Pentheus of the goodness of the Dionysian god, saying that "mankind had two blessings," and one of these is the young god, Dionysus, whom Pentheus is bent on destroying. Tiresias also attempts to reassure the king about the supposedly lewd nature of the festival, claiming that:

It's not for Dionysus to make women modest.
Foolproof chastity depends on character,
and in the corybantic celebrations
no decent woman is seduced.

The play's ending clearly states the Athenian view of the Dionysian cult, as Pentheus' mother, Agave, who has joined the Bacchantes, tears apart her own son while possessed by the Dionysian frenzy. It is plain that for Euripides and his audience, the dance of the Bacchae represented a dangerous force to the Greek state. Women who were called by the god readily abandoned their household duties to form bands of wild dancers roving the mountainsides, thoughtlessly murdering their children and jeopardizing the male citizenry's right to legitimate heirs. Clearly, the state could not tolerate a ritual which encouraged women to leave their homes and engage in pleasures usually reserved for men. Nor could it permit women to freely exercise their sexuality.

In actual fact, the Dionysian "frenzies" associated with ancient matrilineal cults of the great goddess were forced by statesmen into acceptable political formats. The rituals were driven into state-approved festivals and eventually formed the Greek theatre, where the disorderly energy of the body was ordered along precise dramatic lines and contained in a performance space which established clear boundaries between spectators and participants. As for women, their presence as participants was not permitted; men played women's roles in Athenian drama. It is not known if women were permitted to attend the ceremonies even as spectators.

Though women were isolated in the household where they were deprived of contact with a community of peers, and their movement was severely restricted, they continued to dance in the privacy of their homes and in state-approved festivals. In their homes, women celebrated birth dances on rooftops on the tenth day after a child's birth; in public, they performed lamentations of the dead and danced at wedding festivities; they also performed various fertility and harvest dances at ordained state festivities. Slaves and lower class women also danced professionally as entertainers and prostitutes, performing lewd dances for men. The dances performed by courtesans derived their names from a kneading-trough, tub, or a mortar, and they involved a rotating motion of the hips and abdomen, movements which originated in the fertility rites once considered sacred and performed in honour of the great goddess.

These dances retained some of the outer trappings of women's former rituals and some of women's traditional concern for the body, but their significance was publicly determined by the patriarchal state. With the appearance and movements of their bodies legislated by the male state, and their energy colonized to maintain approved lines of patriarchy, what, if anything but the barest outline, remains of women in these state-approved gestures?

2. ISADORA DUNCAN: FREEING THE BODY

Isadora Duncan's revolutionary work in dance, started in America at the beginning of the twentieth century, was inspired by the gesture of the Maenads outlawed by the patriarchal Greek state of the fifth century B.C.E. Isadora, who studied the figures of dancing Maenads drawn on Greek vases, believed that the characteristic gesture of the dancing Maenad, with her head thrown back in ecstasy, epitomized a movement of the spirit fully alive and abundantly flowing from the body.

> This figure is the best example I could give of an emotion taking entire possession of the body. The head is turned backward— but the movement of the head is not calculated; it is the result of the overwhelming feeling of Dionysiac ecstasy which is portrayed in the entire body.

In the Duncan lexicon, this gesture represents a perfect dance movement, where the natural movement of the body emanates from the spirit, marking a moment in which the body can no longer contain the exuberance of the spirit and finally lets itself be carried by an impulse it can no longer resist. It is not the gesture itself, but the power and truth of the spirit behind the gesture which so inspired Duncan in her work, as she pursued her belief in dance as the art of finding the "motor of the soul" which stirs the whole body to knowledge of its natural movements.

Duncan's work was bound to the work of building healthy female bodies and reclaiming the creativity of women. "If my art is symbolic of any one thing, it is symbolic of the freedom of women," she commented in a newspaper interview in 1922. This comment is particularly significant as it was made in light of Boston Mayor Curley's ban against Isadora's further performances in that city on the charge that she had indecently exposed herself on stage. During this same tour, Isadora performed in Indianapolis with two policemen on stage, who were responsible for ensuring that the dancer's body remain covered at all times. The police presence was requested by Lew Shanks, mayor of Indianapolis, who gave this assessment of Isadora's art to the press:

> Isadora ain't foolin' me any. She talks about art. Huh! I've seen a lot of these twisters and I know as much about art as any man in America, but I never went to see these dancers for art's sake. No, sir, I'll bet that ninety percent of men who go to those so-called classical dancers just say they think it's artistic to fool their wives... No sir, these nude dancers don't get by me. If she goes pulling off her clothes and throwin' them in the air, as she is said to have done in Boston, there's going to be somebody getting a ride in the wagon.

Throughout her career, Isadora Duncan was faced with censorship of this kind. In an earlier tour, the pastors of the Methodist Episcopal Church in St. Louis overwhelmingly passed a resolution condemning her performances as "the grossest violation of the proprieties of life," and she was denounced in a sermon from the pulpit by a Dr. Thompson, who accused her of being a menace to the nation.

> But it is to St. Louis' shame that following after came the spectacle of last Tuesday evening in the Coliseum. To her shame that such an exhibition was possible in her midst; that such an audience could be so affronted; that an orchestra second to few in the world should consent to be merely a background for plain and ill-disguised nudity; that Beethoven's stately symphony should be so degraded; that before the very flower of this queenly city dances should be performed that if given in other sections of the city and under other conditions would be promptly suppressed by the police.
>
> And the excuse for it all is art— high art; as though art could consecrate nastiness. One of your art reporters in describing the evening said of the dancing: "It was the happiness of the physically perfect young animal." But it was not a young animal that danced, but

a middle-aged woman who has been for years associated with the Parisian stage.

Isadora is accused of the most dangerous crime a woman can commit in patriarchy— owning her body in private and in public, in love and in work. The reaction of these men in power is indicative of how her lived idea of freedom for women conflicted with and threatened the patriarchal seal on the body. The rhetoric of censorship, the police presence, and the church's denunciation conceal an idea and law of the body which dictates how, where, and why women may move. Isadora did not fit this model. As Isadora herself observed in an interview, the issue was not nudity:

> Surely it is not more indecent than the sight of forty girls in flesh-coloured drawers dancing the "can can" on your vaudeville stage. That may be seen any day.

The issue was her explicitly stated intention to free women's bodies from the constraints of morality and fashion and the fact that she used her body to satisfy her private inner visions and not the male eye.

A free body was essential to Isadora's vision of dance; in her view, the return of women's "original strength" and the "natural movements of women's body" were inseparable from the evolution of dance as an art form. Dance was the expression of the body's natural inclination to beauty and was not idealized in particular forms. Its highest ideal, Beauty, appeared wherever the dynamic embodiment of inner and outer realities formed an unencumbered continuum:

> I prefer the movement of a hunchback inspired by an inner idea to the coquettish, graceful, though effective gesture of a beautiful woman. There is no pose, no movement, no gesture that is beautiful in itself. Every movement is beautiful only when it is expressed truthfully and sincerely.

To fulfil this ideal, everything about the female body had to be changed, including diet and dress. When Isadora saw the full lines of movement depicted in the statues of dancing Maenads she recognized how deformed women's bodies had become in dance and everyday life, and how alienated women were from the truth of their bodies. Fashion represented a state of imprisonment, where women, besieged by corsets, tight shoes, and heavy layers of clothing, could not listen to their bodies and dance truthfully from the spirit. To counteract the suffocating effects of fashion, Isadora adopted a dress which allowed the body to breathe and move freely. On stage and in her private life she wore free-flowing tunics and shawls or simply designed dresses, while on her feet she wore sandals or went barefoot. This same dress was adopted by her pupils. One of them, Irma Duncan, remembers the liberating effect she felt the first time she exchanged her tight clothes for the costume devised by Duncan:

> I distinctly recall the sense of freedom I experienced in those light and simple clothes, which were the distinctive Duncan uniform and which would henceforth set us apart from other people.

(In 1989, I attended the screening of a video on Isadora Duncan, where an elderly woman in the audience spoke of her training as a Duncan dancer. After all these years, she also remembered the costume's liberating effect. "You have to understand," she said, plucking the shoulder of her dress, "as a young girl, to be dressed like that, so free, to do those movements. For a young girl at that time it was so freeing.")

As metaphor and fact, fashion operates as a practical instrument of control over women's bodies. The clothing women wore at the beginning of the twentieth century hampered their movements and breathing, debilitated and weakened their health, and directed their movements along tightly ordered lines, reinforcing the image of women as frail, weak, and passive. Isadora understood this perfectly, and insisted that all her pupils be clothed in loose and comfortable tunics to allow them to spontaneously feel the movements of their limbs and the effects of breathing deeply and moving energetically. Layer by layer, Isadora meant to remove all the conventions that conspired to keep the female body from its source of freely determined movements and natural desires and ultimately from knowledge of its own creative potential.

> First draw me the form of a woman as it is in Nature. And now draw me the form of a woman in a modern corset and the satin slippers used by our modern dancers. Now do you not see that the movement that would conform to one figure would be perfectly impossible for the other? To the first all the rhythmic movements that run through Nature would be possible. They would find this form their natural medium for movement. To the second figure these movements would be impossible on account of the rhythm being broken, and stopped at the extremities.

Isadora's concept of dance was far removed from prevailing stage dances of the music-hall type with the "kicks and frills" she had rejected early on in her career, and with the ballet, which she saw as calculated steps and patterns performed by deformed bodies for the enjoyment of balletomanes. The past two thousand years had seen a degeneration of the dance which she vowed to overturn by returning to the natural movements of the body, freed from commercialization and the external constraints of fashion and morality. She was thoroughly convinced that dance would remain an empty, commercialized venture until the female body was freed of these restrictions, both on stage and in everyday life.

Isadora's criticism of the ballet focused on the unnaturalness of the balletic line and the unnatural formation of the female body in toe shoes and corseted costumes. She urged the public to see beyond the pretty patterns and tutus, into the body of the dancer:

> But look— under the skirts, under the tricots are dancing deformed muscles. Look still farther— underneath the muscles are deformed bones. A deformed skeleton is dancing before you. This deformation

through incorrect dress and incorrect movement is the result of the
training necessary to the ballet.

The ballet condemns itself by enforcing the deformation of the
beautiful woman's body!

Her criticism of ballet was not simply based on an aesthetic disagree-
ment, but revolved around the larger question of the use and value of
the female body and the democratic right to educate the body to its own
movements. In the formation of the balletic body, the dancer, who
aspired to the suspension of belief in the natural law of gravity, went
against the body and against nature. As a result, the natural sequence of
her movements was arrested, isolated in space and time, transforming
her dance into the static offering of her body to the audience.

In the nineteenth and early twentieth centuries, ballet had become
a showcase of women where balletic costumes and movements cut up
the female body purely for purposes of display. The balletic form
interrupted or disregarded the internal rhythm of the dancer and dissected
her movements into poses which best displayed her body to the male
theatre-goer. Isadora reversed this order by instituting a dance training
which insisted that the dancer listen to her body to find the initiating and
sustaining pulse of her movements. She removed the external eye from
the dancer's consciousness— her students never practised before mirrors— and returned the impulse of movement to the centre of the body
where the dancer assumed responsibility for the evolution of its form.
The differences between ballet and Isadora's new dance were evident in
the line and carriage of the body and the style and intention of movement,
but the real difference lay in the fact that Isadora valued an autonomous
and creative female self and welcomed the visions generated by the
female artist.

Isadora adamantly maintained that the regeneration of dance was one
with the regeneration of the female body. Beneath this conviction, there
is a clear-sighted appreciation of the historical continuity of women in
dance and the bond sealed by women in the body. Isadora's ideal of

Greek beauty focused on a figure which the classical Greeks repudiated as unpolitical, that is, unpatriarchal. While the Greeks outlawed the Maenads and absorbed their energy into the classical Greek stage, Isadora Duncan stood on this same stage two thousand years later and reversed the law of patriarchy by opening up the territory of the female body. And like the Maenads' dance, hers also was rooted in nature and ritual.

In her choreography, her teachings, and writings on dance, Isadora returned again and again to the idea that dance begins in nature. In an essay entitled "The Dancer and Nature" Isadora wrote that:

> Woman is not a thing apart and separate from all other life organic and inorganic. She is but a link in the chain, and her movement must be one with the great movement which runs through the universe; and therefore the fountain-head for the art of the dance will be the study of the movements of Nature.

True dance comes from the patterns of nature in which Isadora saw a distilled wave movement running through all natural phenomena, including the human body. This wave movement was created by the alternating current of gravity in its attraction and resistance to matter which the dancer concentrated in the place or site of the body, thus explaining the need to release the body from all artificially imposed restrictions. This perception of the dancer as a part of nature, capable of channelling nature into creative human expression, philosophically contradicted the idea of humans as beings set apart from nature and endowed with a god-given right to dominate nature. Duncan's dancer accepts her place in nature and opens herself to its forces, to translate the knowledge of nature passing through her, taking up the philosophical thread of the matriarchal world which also processed the forces of nature in the interest of the body.

In her autobiography, Isadora describes how she came to identify and refine the ability to sense the impulse of natural movement in the body, starting with a quiet and patient reflection from the body:

I spent long days and nights in the studio seeking that dance which might be the divine expression of the human spirit through the medium of the body's movement. For hours I would stand quite still, my two hands folded between my breasts, covering the solar plexus. My mother often became alarmed to see me remain for such long intervals quite motionless as if in a trance— but I was seeking and finally discovered the central spring of all movement, the crater of motor power, the unity from which all diversities of movements are born, the mirror of vision for the creation of the dance— it was from this discovery that was born the theory on which I founded my school.

From this simple and private beginning Isadora developed a fluid and inspired theory of movement. Those who saw her dance were struck by the spontaneity and self-abandonment of her dances, sometimes glossing over the technique which went into the articulation of her movements. In a sense, Isadora encouraged this view by declaring her art a religion, her dance a prayer emanating from the soul, capable of breaking barriers between the spectator as passive recipient and the dancer as active messenger. Isadora did not want her audiences only to be stimulated visually, she wanted them to also feel and act upon the great forces transpiring in her. The design of the stage space frustrated her desire for a more complete expression in which the body of the dancer and the audience would be released from prescriptive spaces and designs.

But I have dreamed of a more complete dance expression on the part of the audience, at a theatre in the form of an amphitheatre, where there would be no reason why, at certain times, the public should not arise and, by different gestures of dance, participate in my invocation.

In her art, Isadora founded a new dance form that valued the private vision of the female artist and established women's creativity within a historical context. This sense of history also enabled her to look to the future and fuelled her vision of a school in which thousands of young girls would be educated to the intelligence of their bodies. "A free spirit in a free body"— this was the motto of the Duncan school and an abbreviated version of the lesson which Isadora hoped to instill in future generations. Irma Duncan, the disciple, who worked alongside Isadora to realize the idea of the school, remarks that:

> I know of no other precedent in modern times where a young artist, at the start of a promising career, is moved to invest hard-won earnings in a philanthropical enterprise simply to gratify some lofty ideal. But Isadora Duncan did just that. Rather than invest her money in diamonds and costly furs and expensive mansions and other luxuries so many women crave, she spent every penny she earned on the upkeep of her school.

It was in trying to establish her school that Isadora most clearly saw and experienced society's resistance to the idea and fact of the free female body. From the beginning of her career to her death in 1927, Isadora travelled Europe and America with one idea in mind. She intended to find a place where, aided by government or public funds, she could support her vision of educating children to be independent and creative.

Over the years, Isadora used funds earned through touring to establish schools in Germany, France, America, and Russia. Though she struggled, the cost of housing, feeding, and educating her students was high; she could not provide all the necessary funds by herself, and one by one the schools closed. As a school closed in one country it brought to life the dream of opening it in another. Isadora never lost faith in the idea of her school, though she once commented wearily on the string of failures caused by the lack of public support:

> When I was twenty-one, I offered my School to Germany. The

Kaiserin responded that it was immoral! The Kaiser said it was revolutionary! Then I proposed my School to America, but they said there that it stood for the vine, and Dionysus... I then proposed my School to Greece, but the Greeks were too busy fighting the Turks. Today I propose my School to France, but France, in the person of the amiable Minister of Fine Arts, gives me a smile. I cannot nourish the children in my School on a smile.

After France's refusal of aid in 1920, post-revolutionary Russia responded to Isadora's dream of establishing a permanent school and invited her to Moscow with the promise of a building and financial support. Isadora accepted and with the help of Irma Duncan established a school which remained open for a total of seven years before collapsing under economic pressure and government interference.

Whatever country she was in, Isadora opened her schools to the most disenfranchised populations of children, poor children and orphans who could not otherwise afford the education she so generously provided for them. Isadora accepted complete responsibility for the students of her schools, paying the full cost of feeding, housing, clothing, and educating the girls who came to her. She accepted no tuition and the enormity of her responsibilities and fierceness of her desire can best be judged from that fact that at the age of twenty-eight she accepted full financial responsibility for the twenty children enrolled in her first school in Grunewald, a suburb of Berlin. In post-revolutionary Russia, Isadora believed that she had finally found a government which supported her view of free education for children of all classes, but this school also succumbed to a lack of money and ideological differences, as the government insisted the school shift its focus to developing physical culture and muscular strength, an emphasis which Isadora had always resisted in dance. Isadora's dancer of the future was a woman devoted to beauty and the soul. Not bound by nationality, she belonged to all of humanity, though it seems no nation wanted to risk educating her and then having to deal with her as a citizen.

Of all the rejections experienced in her career, Isadora most bitterly took to heart America's rejection of her art and school. Early in her career, she firmly contradicted critics who labelled her dance as "the revival of classical Greek dance," assuring them that her dance, though inspired by ancient art forms, was unmistakably modern and American in nature. Like Walt Whitman's vision of America singing, Isadora also had a vision of America:

> I see America dancing, beautiful, strong, with one foot poised on the highest point of the Rockies, her two hands stretched out from the Atlantic to the Pacific, her fine head tossed to the sky, her forehead shining with a crown of a million stars.

By stressing the modernity of her art and its relevance to her contemporaries, Isadora resisted the potential disempowerment of her ideas by those who removed them to the distant past. Her art was about freedom of the body and freedom of women and she meant those freedoms to be taken up in her time, not displayed in a glass case as quaint revivals of ancient and inoffensive forms.

Isadora's art was tied to the condition of women, as was the censorship and lack of support she endured. In the same speech in which she denounced censorship in the arts and America's indifference to the condition of her artists, Isadora spoke of the detrimental effects of marriage on women. She insisted on a woman's right to bear children with whomever she chose, a right which Isadora exercised in her own life, giving birth to children by men whom she refused to marry. Isadora fully recognized that a woman could not be free only on stage or in the confines of her art. Her freedom had also to be lived in everyday life and in every aspect of her creative being. This assertion of a woman's complete right to her body and her creativity, including reproductive powers, seriously threatened societies and governments built on the colonization of women's productive and reproductive labour. Isadora's commitment to women's freedom was a complete expression of art and life lived in the body. She recognized the continuity between art and life and the relation between freedom and the body and so drew resistance from the state, the clergy, the police— all representations of power in male society and the moral and divisive wall of force which defends the rights of all men over women's movements.

Isadora's accusations against America— that America lacked imagination and starved and persecuted her artists— indicates the long history and acceptance of censorship in the arts in America, particularly when the subject is the body. Isadora's art released the power and imagination of the body into everyday life, crossing carefully drawn lines between law and desire and blotting out the code of acceptable moral behaviour enforced in women's personalities. Fundamentally, the attacks against her art were aimed at the body and at protecting an idea of the body, molded over the centuries, in which there is no place for the fact and image of a female body released from male control.

By herself and in her own way, Isadora understood many of the things which have again become clear to women in the past twenty-five years— the necessity of a healthy body, the right to freely determine our creative and procreative resources, the obligation to study our history as women and prepare for the future, and the power and intelligence of the body. I think the following encounter, laughingly remembered by Isadora, epitomizes the power of a free woman dancing for herself in the tradition of her ancestresses:

I always wanted to find out how the ancient Greeks managed to dance the ten kilometres during the great festival of the Eleusinian Mysteries. One day I got up at five o'clock in the morning after making up my mind to dance that distance myself in a light tunic. I was dancing along the highway when I noticed that I was approaching a Greek priest who was breakfasting at the side of the road. Seeing the dancing and apparently resurrected Maenad, the priest looked at me with wide-open, frightened eyes and, flinging his staff on to the grass, hitched up the skirts of his cassock and ran away from me at such a speed that even a Maenad could not have overtaken him. He ruined my test, for I could not help stopping and laughing my head off. But that merely quickened his run.

3. BALLET MASTERS: COLONIZING THE BODY

Isadora's deep listening to the body brought her to a physical expression which picked up the gestures of women interrupted by the patriarchal state. Taking on the gesture of the Maenads, frozen in mid-sentence, Isadora developed it into a form which accepted the voice of the body as an inspirational force. Movement was no longer dictated from the mind and imposed by will on the body's musculature; it arose from within, filling the body with meaning. This new dance form meant a whole rethinking and reshaping of the female body, internally and externally, as the body's intelligence and sustaining images were given room to resurface from decades of repression. This way of working from within the body generated a movement which differed from prevailing dance styles of the times, particularly ballet.

Classical ballet most clearly articulates in narrative and technique the ideology of patriarchy in dance and its effect on the female body, showing the ways in which the dancer is isolated in her power and appropriated by men as spectators and choreographers. In this tradition, a colonized body works out the controlled expenditure of its own resources according to a patriarchally inscribed ritual in which the power of the female body, displaced by an internalized and centralized male ideal, is marginalized in itself.

In an interview during the film *The Second Sex*, a young ballet dancer from the Paris Opera summed up her work as a dancer with the following statement:

As dancers, our goal is to represent men's ideal.

Defining the ideal goal of the woman dancer as the representation of a male ideal replicates on stage the power relation between men and women defined outside the sphere of dance. Patriarchy as philosophy and cultural institution is built on the theory and practice of power over women and the culture of the maternal body. Accepting the power of the male imagination as the directive force of the body on stage is another instance of this exercise in power over women and it is both aesthetic and political.

Classical ballet encourages this abdication of power by offering tightly circumscribed roles for women dancers. As Sleeping Beauty, Giselle, Odette, or Odile the ballerina is caught in a romanticized idealization of women. There is an apparent contradiction in this dynamic arising from the fact that the ballerina expends a tremendous amount of energy to sustain this view of her ultimate powerlessness. Like the model in art history, the ballerina invests her creativity, her time, and her body in satisfying and realizing a male ideal of sexual desire predicated on female powerlessness. The historical significance of model and dancer come together as one in the work of Edgar Degas, described by his contemporaries and art historians as the painter of ballet dancers.

In a letter to a friend, Degas refuted his ascribed role as a painter of ballet dancers, writing that, for him, the dancers exist only as "a pretext for painting pretty materials and delineating movement." With this bald reduction of the dancer to the gauze and tulle of a costume and to lines in space, it is not surprising to find out that all of Degas' dancers remain anonymous. We do not know these women by name, although we do know the name of the ballet master who appears with them in several of the paintings. And of course we know the name of the painter who represented them.

Though Degas denies seeing the dancer as an individual and professes to paint only abstract colours, shapes, and forms, he does establish relations between the people in his paintings. These relations, for the most part, maintain the narrative structure of male dominance over the female body and the subservience of women's artistic enterprise to a male standard and vision. The painting "The Star," from 1875, subtly illustrates this. The star is a ballet dancer extended in a generous arabesque; she is pictured alone down centre stage. In the wings, stage right, Degas has painted the corps de ballet in a flurry of colours in which only vague shapes are discernible, with here and there the addition of a pair of legs or a ballet shoe. Down stage of the corps, and partially hidden by a painted flat, we see a male figure in evening dress. His face and part of his upper torso are hidden behind the flat but we know that he is looking at the star. In contrast to the star, who is perched on one leg, his feet are set apart in a solid proprietary stance. The star's attention is completely focused forward on the audience before her and there is nothing in her facial expression or body posture to indicate that she realizes she is also being watched from behind.

Degas drew his model dancers from the Paris Opera during a time in which ballet had become a minor form of entertainment. By the late nineteenth century, ballet no longer formed a part of operatic spectacles and was attended by *abonnés*, men who held season tickets and who, according to a French journalist, frequented the ballet "almost as they frequent certain other places of easier access," in reference to brothels. Many of these men were members of the Jockey Club, an exclusive private club of horse breeders, and they treated the ballet as a private showcase from which to choose their evening's real entertainment, which began after the show. Dance historian Ivor Guest comments that the members of the Jockey Club regarded the Opera as a sort of "fief" or "private seraglio" and quotes from a nineteenth century commentator who observed that the Opera provided Jockey Club members "with their amorous pleasures, just as the Pompadour stud-farm provides them with their equestrian pleasures; they consider it as a storehouse of remounts, no more."

The shadowy male figure in "The Star" establishes the proprietary relation described by Guest. By inserting this figure in the background, Degas reminds us that the star does not belong to herself and he robs us of the pleasure of her movement. When we blot out this figure, a completely different picture emerges, and the painting becomes the representation of a woman at work, luxuriating in the extension of her body and the achievement of technical proficiency as she reaches out to her audience. The removal of the male figure from the scene banishes the voyeuristic gaze that holds the dancer still, and restores the movement in her body. With no one in the wings waiting to claim her, the viewer, like the dancer, is no longer confined by a reading of the female body determined by male desire.

The shadowy male presence exists in many other Degas paintings: "Ballet rehearsal on the stage, 1878-79," "Rehearsal of a ballet on the stage, 1874," "Dancers backstage, 1872," and "The Curtain," among others. In this body of work, the men are points of stillness in paintings otherwise filled with movement— stretches, arabesques, pirouettes, extensions— and often they are the only non-dancers in the paintings. Their role is to look and to ensure by example a reading of the dancer which places women in the conventional role of sexual object and affirms men's ownership over women's creativity.

In many of the paintings the voyeuristic look serves to draw together the different elements within the frame. When this look is removed, it becomes an effort to relate the figures, and it becomes apparent that though Degas depicts women in groups involved in a common activity, the female figures hardly ever relate to each other: they do not touch each other, they do not look at each other, and they do not fix each other's costumes or groom each other in any way. For the most part, the dancers are either absorbed in their own bodies— examining their feet, rubbing an ankle, adjusting a costume, yawning, or scratching them-selves— or their attention is turned toward the male figure in the painting— the ballet master, the musician, or the gentleman in evening clothes. Consequently, when we blot out the male figures, the paintings lose their narrative structure and the ballet dancers appear to be wander-ing aimlessly or pointing with legs and arms to empty space. It becomes clear that their movements and their activity are determined by a male presence. These are women at work, but men still give their work meaning; even in private moments of rehearsing, grooming, studying, and relaxing, Degas assures us that women do not own themselves nor do they create bonds between each other.

The appropriation of the product of the dancer's body and skills occurs along with the appropriation of her creative process. In the painting "The Ballet Rehearsal," from 1875, Degas fuses the appropriation of product and process into a single image, by presenting both the ballet master and an anonymous patron in an apparent exchange over a young ballet dancer. The ballet master, framed by three other dancers, stands to one side of the scene. In his left hand he holds a stout staff, the traditional sign of male authority. His right hand is extended forward in a gesture of offering and display. The object of the gesture is a young ballet dancer on pointe, her body slightly turned and her right hand pointing upward as her eyes follow the gesture into space. On the other side of the scene, and apparently unnoticed by the ballet dancer on pointe, Degas has painted a male figure in evening dress whose body is partially cut off by the edge of the painting. The ballet master seems to be offering up his creation to this gentleman.

In this painting, Degas has cast the ballet master in the role of a pimp offering a prostitute to a client. The prostitute/dancer engaged in her movement is oblivious to her fate. She is a finished product ready for consumption and the ballet master who shaped her body to accommodate male pleasure assumes the power of giving her away. This exchange is based on a fundamental agreement between the ballet master and the patron with regard to the construction of male desire and its idealized form in the female body. And it calls into question the ballet master's artistic intent. From this scene, it is clear that the dancer is a sexual object for both choreographer and spectator. Neither of these men perceive the dancer as a creative artist capable of using the material of her body to project a private vision. Nor does the ballet master aspire to a creative ideal beyond the principle and construction of male pleasure. Here there is a complete identification of creativity with male desire and a tidy picture of the cycle of production and exchange operative in the patriarchal world of dance. The power of the female body is made to exist and circulate within this tightly circumscribed circle of exchange between men. The ballet dancer exposed to the male look and vision does not openly challenge the assumption of power over her body, though she does contain and maintain the power in her body. Her look, focused on a male presence or searching space, indicates that she is unconscious of the power in her body and removed from the transformative urge to change this power into a female-defined vision.

The elements of power and the sexual politics depicted in Degas' work remain a part of contemporary Western dance culture in classical ballet. In the twentieth century, the power of men and the disempowerment of women is evident still in the relations between choreographer and dancer and in concentrated attempts by choreographers and critics to place male dancers in positions of superiority.

George Balanchine, the late choreographer of the New York City Ballet and the most influential ballet choreographer of the twentieth century asserted that

> the ballet is a purely female thing; it is a garden of beautiful flowers and the man is the gardener.

This statement is often quoted to illustrate Balanchine's great love of women and the ballet, but the assumptions of power beneath this view are hardly flattering to women or useful to the development of ballet. In this view, the relation between choreographer and dancer parallels the established relation of man and nature in patriarchal thought. The flower/dancer is identified with a passive nature, trained to serve the aesthetic ideal of the male gardener, who owns the means of consciously creating her. Here again, the flower/dancer is unconscious of the power in her body which must wait on the male gardener/choreographer to transform her into an object of value. In another, related, statement, Balanchine elaborates on his gardening analogy, saying that:

When you have a garden full of pretty flowers, you don't demand of them, "What do you mean? What is your significance?" You just enjoy them.

From this statement it is clear that the choreographer is not concerned with the meaning of the female body, spirit, mind, or imagination. The choreographer is concerned with pleasing the male eye and satisfying his demand for young, white, and thin female bodies. In this context, the enjoyment of dance is predicated on the erasure of the female as subject and the manipulation of her body from a very early age.

The disempowerment of women as a condition for the creation of art was worked out in one of Balanchine's first works, choreographed before his arrival in the United States, where he was given the responsibility of developing a distinctly American ballet style. The ballet, originally called *Apollon Musagete*, was later referred to as *Apollo* or *Apollo, Leader of the Muses*, and is set to music by Igor Stravinsky. It was premiered on April 27, 1937, at the Metropolitan Opera House in New York, and was a revival from the Diaghilev Ballets Russes where Balanchine had choreographed the work in 1928 for the dancer Serge Lifar. The ballet, whose principal role was coveted by leading male dancers, is still performed as part of the New York City Ballet's repertoire.

Apollo describes the relation between the god Apollo and the three muses, Calliope as poetry and rhythm, Polyhymnia as mime, and Terpsichore as rhythm and gesture. Lincoln Kirstein, in his memoirs of the New York City Ballet, describes the ballet in words that expose the sexual politics at work between Apollo and the muses:

In its grave sequence Balanchine carved four cameos in three dimensions. Calliope portrayed the metric and caesura of spoken verse; Polyhymnia described mimicry and spectacular gesture; Terpsichore, the activity, declaration, and inversion of academic dancing itself. *These are all subservient to Apollo, animator and driver;*

they are his handmaidens, creatures, harem, and household. He is the dance
master whose authority develops from boy to man to god. Freed from
swaddling bands, he feels and flexes muscle, matures into manhood,
chooses his foredestined partner; finally assumes his godhead. The
muses do not develop; they move in a temporal element which has
no history, fixed in their idealized preordained powers. [Emphasis
mine.]

In *Apollo*, Balanchine choreographed clear demarcations of power
and a gender-based stratification of the creative impulse, which glorifies
the male principle as supreme creator whose role it is to dominate and
"drive" the female personified in the muses. In the ballet, each of the
muses takes a turn dancing before Apollo, seeking his approval and the
prize of his love. When Apollo dances for the muses, the meaning of his
dance is quite different. He dances to remind the muses of his ideal
perfection and of his superiority in art. The muses offer themselves to
him, act horrified when they commit an error of gesture which dimin-
ishes them in Apollo's eyes, and finally are literally driven across the stage
by Apollo in a series of gestures which creates the illusion of a chariot
drawn by females whipped and driven by a male figure.

From the primary assumption that power and art relate to sex,
Balanchine draws a number of others: all creativity derives from the male
principle; the male alone is perfect and in command of all arts— the
muses are at best fragmentary representations of knowledge already
possessed by the male; the male has absolute decision making power over
the value of women's art; the male is the true teacher and he alone is
capable of development and change; the interest of women in art is to
gain the love of a man; and the muses do not work together but compete
for the love of a man/god.

The idealization of the male figure in Balanchine's ballet and the
consequent dismissal of power in the female body is brought to its logical
conclusion in the works and aesthetic of Maurice Béjart, choreographer
of Les Ballets Béjart in Belgium. Béjart, who is known for his almost

exclusive use of male dancers, responded to Balanchine's gardening analogy with his own comment on the sexual nature of dance:

> That may be true. But then dance is man!... My basis for this statement is in the facts of folklore. Popular traditions show that more often than not man is the one who dances; he is the best dancer.

Béjart's sentiments are supported by critics Alexander Bland and John Percival, in their book entitled *Men Dancing*. Bland and Percival also claim men's natural superiority in dance, basing it in instinct:

> ... human instinct probably divided men from women at certain moments, giving special prominence— and so special dance movements— to selected individuals. These were usually men, one reason being that the athletic male body is best equipped for the violent activities thought to be needed to attract human or divine attention. In the oldest of arts, men held first place.

Elaborating on the idea of male supremacy in dance, Bland and Percival go on to observe that when women do dance, their participation leads to a degeneration of the art. In their words, dance becomes "effeminate." Happily they conclude that through the efforts of superstars such as Nureyev and Baryshnikov men have rescued Terpischore from this fate. They measure the extent of this success economically, through box office receipts, which prove

> that men have won back their honourable status and in so doing [have] added strength, solidity, and breadth to an art always on the brink of dwindling into specialized or trivial charm. The effeminate, elitist image of dance has disappeared.

These views are a distillation of Balanchine's aesthetic, which maintains a controlled and token feminine presence designed to serve male visions of power and creativity. Whether the female dancer is fetishized in a flowery cult of beauty and romance or entirely removed from the stage space, her position is determined by the equation of power and creativity with men, violence, and money.

INSTINCTS
FOR
DANCE

The human body... is a promise of sanity.
Adrian Stokes

The impulse to rethink the body is not restricted to dancers for whom the body is the principle source and means of expression. Artists in other fields have also struggled with the necessity of reinterpreting the body as a condition for continued survival and creativity. In this section I would like to look at one painter and two writers for whom the body and dance have been central: Leonora Carrington, Zelda Fitzgerald, and H.D. For each of these women the body becomes a protected place of discovery, comfort, and sanity. And for each of them dance is, in one sense or another, a way of entering into the body and a way of making or interpreting a renewed relation to the self.

1. LEONORA CARRINGTON: DOWN BELOW

Leonora Carrington is a surrealist painter and writer. Like the dancer Isadora Duncan, she found it necessary to re-examine and shift the balance lived in her body. While Duncan's work centred on the spirit in relation to the body, Carrington's revolved on the relation between mind and body, which she magnified to include the natural world. For Carrington, effecting a visceral change in habit, posture, thought, and attitude was very much a matter of survival and it did not occur in private, nor was it passed over by society. During the period in which she was trying to resolve this anguish about her mind and her body

Carrington was incarcerated in an insane asylum in Spain in 1941. Later, she wrote about this period in her life in *Down Below*, published in a 1944 issue of the surrealist review *VVV*. This account of her internment raises questions about the regulation of the body, insanity, feminine consciousness, and the order of patriarchal law founded in the body.

Leonora Carrington was born in 1917 into a wealthy family in England where her father was president of the Imperial Chemical Industries conglomerate. Carrington attended schools in Florence, Paris, and London where, at the age of twenty, she met the surrealist painter Max Ernst whom she accompanied to Paris. In Paris, Carrington was favourably received by other members of the surrealist movement, including André Breton, and exhibited paintings in their group shows. Carrington remained in France until the events of World War II forced her to flee to Spain, where she was incarcerated in an insane asylum at Santander on the Basque Coast. After her release from the asylum, Carrington fled to Portugal, where she remained until a Mexican diplomat offered to marry her to assist her escape from Europe. Carrington accepted and the couple moved first to New York, then Mexico. This marriage was shortly dissolved and Carrington later remarried and gave birth to two sons. Since 1942, she has made Mexico her home, and over the years has continued to paint and write while becoming an active member of the women's movement in Mexico.

Carrington is associated with the surrealist movement, which could claim that "*la révolution est femme*," while maintaining the same image of women as the bourgeois society and art it erected itself against.

> I had noticed with a certain consternation that the place of women among the Surrealists was no different from that which they occupied among the population in general, the bourgeoisie included.

wrote painter Dorothea Tanning. The female body as the projected work of the surrealist imagination was coded in symbols and images carried over from prevailing conservative notions. Though surrealists claimed to be invading and uncovering the uncharted territory of the psyche, stripping it to its barest and socially uncluttered dimension, their work in reality placed women in objectified postures characteristic of patriarchy. The surrealist imagination offered *la femme-poupée*, *la femme-enfant*, and *la femme-fatale* variations of the most conservative ideas of women as virgin/whore. Whether objectified in fetishistic desire, glorified as the personification of male love, or sought after as the mysterious, supernatural other, woman was still perceived as the objectified other and not as an active, autonomous self with imaginative and creative impulses. And it is still her body which is disturbed and made to accept the results of surrealist experiments with non-rational modes of discourse, as if the underside of male reason cannot carry itself to the point of disturbing the male body which alone remains inviolate. In this movement also, women are the carriers of the male imagination, bending their bodies to fit the shape of revolutionary experiments of the mind.

Leonora Carrington's work differs from the surrealist movement with which she is often associated. Her work is deeply female in origin, intent, and outcome. In a commentary published in the catalogue of a retrospective exhibition held in New York City in 1976, Carrington writes:

History has a peculiarity of making gaps whenever they appear convenient. The Bible, like any other history, is full of gaps and peculiarities that only begin to make sense if understood as a covering-up for a very different kind of civilization which had been eliminated. What kind of civilization?

What kind of civilization? Asking this question is like asking what women were like before patriarchy because women indisputably represent one of the largest gaps in history. Carrington is convinced that this other civilization was different from what we know and she makes her own answers from the imagination and scraps of history where women have leaked through the symbolic and social practices of patriarchy. How these civilizations differ can be found in the images, symbols, and associations of her work; why they differ can be found in her identification of the body as a point of origin and medium for knowledge and creativity.

During her life, Leonora Carrington underwent a tremendous visceral change in which she literally reached through the body constructed for her by history to make contact with an earlier version of her female self. This visceral change was a necessary act for leaving the patriarchal state anchored in her body and imagination. Though interpreted as a nervous breakdown, it can also be read as an act of excavation to rid the body and the senses of the internalized patriarchal order.

> The furies, who have a sanctuary buried many fathoms under education and brain washing, have told Females they will return, return from under the fear, shame, and finally through the crack in the prison door, Fury.

wrote Carrington. "The crack in the prison door" is the body, and removing the layers of education and brainwashing to let the furies surface can be a profoundly dangerous experiment.

The forces Carrington worked out through her body were initiated in a kind of mad dance for the recovery of a lost self which she wrote about in *Down Below*. World War II is an important backdrop to the events which occurred in Carrington's life at this time, because it initiated the breakdown which prompted a reorientation of her senses, and because it emphasized the difference between her changed perception of the world and the prevailing ideology of the state occupied with its own frenzied dance of control.

At the onset of the war, Carrington was sharing a house at St. Martin d'Ardèche in the south of France with her lover, the painter Max Ernst.

She dates the beginning of her breakdown to May, 1940, when Max, a German citizen, was taken prisoner by rifle-carrying gendarmes. Left alone to decipher this event and the war that caused it, Carrington spent time thinking about the ills and injustices of society. She eventually found that these wrongs were located within her body, particularly the stomach, which she believed to be the seat of society, "but also the place in which I was united with all the elements of the earth," she says.

When society's madness reaches her, Carrington responds by examining and returning to a primitive relation between her body and food, seeing in this relation a tentative beginning toward an understanding that enfolds all universes, macroscopic and microscopic. In what she views as a necessary first step to purge herself of society's ills, she voluntarily induces vomiting for twenty-four hours. When she begins to eat again, she does so sparingly, carefully avoiding meat and subsisting mostly on potatoes, salad, and wine. While on this regimen, she feels enormous surges of strength and works vigorously on her vines daily, astounding the neighbours by her energy and capacity for work.

The meticulous attention Carrington gives to her body and its relation to food can be mistaken for the actions of a powerless woman faced by insurmountable social forces. As a woman alone she has no power over the political and economic corruption of governments affecting her life and the whole of Europe, so she resorts to controlling the only thing within her reach— her body— successfully deluding herself with feelings of strength. Though a valid interpretation, I do not believe it to be the most accurate nor the most informative. It is consistent with the experience of women who suffer from eating disorders and whose sometimes deadly obsessions with food are the means of asserting individual control in a world in which they otherwise feel powerless and out of control, but Carrington's actions have a different sense in that she is not substituting her body for the world, but is entering through her body a sensed continuity between herself and the earth, an experience which challenges the long standing dominant ideologies of male dualistic thought evident all around her in the deadly machinations of war.

Later, during a pause in her story, Carrington suggests that "Reason must know the heart's reason and all the other reasons which are felt from the tip of one's hair to the extremity of one's toes." This reflection is central to her motivation of understanding the world, first in the body, through its simplest and most primary experiences. In order to undo the dominance of a reason predicated on the isolation of the individual in systems of abstraction, Carrington initiates her own search into the nature and place of the individual with the intent of making, not severing, connections. These efforts to unravel reason begin in the body, which solitary theories of reason have consistently denied, misunderstood, and dismissed as a source of intelligence. In contrast to these theories, Carrington begins by accepting her connection with the earth originating in the functioning of the body and its necessity for food. In working her vines, she acts in solidarity with a female centred tradition of tending to the life of the body through cultivation of the earth. And in nurturing her body by attending to the details of her digestion she is beginning a deep listening of the body to clear a space for the life-giving impulses which alone can undo the destructive forces coming at her from the world outside. Many years later Carrington uses the phrase "mak[ing] some interior space for digestive purposes" to describe turning the self inside out to come out from under centuries of false information. It is an apt description of the process she began in 1940.

In these first sustained moments of clarity which come to her from a place below reason, Carrington feels no fear from the events around her, though she is accused of spying by soldiers who threaten to shoot her. This initial well-being passes away as she intensifies her identification with the world and becomes more conscious of the external forces around her. Fear begins to grow in her during a conversation with a woman friend who is obsessed by the possibility of rape. Carrington herself, who most fears "the thought of automatons, of thoughtless, fleshless beings," is eventually persuaded to flee the advancing army of Germans and agrees to accompany her friends to Spain, a trip which to her represents discovery more than escape. However, during the trip she is "jammed" (her words) by anxiety, and by the time they reach the Spanish border she has lost control over her body's movements. As she and her friends wait at the border for their visas, Carrington confronts this loss of motion by renewing her identification with the external world, gradually building up a new entente between her mind, her body, and her world. The following is her description of her paralysis and the way in which she overcomes it:

> When we reached Andorra, I could not walk straight. I walked like a crab; I had lost control over my motions: an attempt at climbing stairs would again bring about a "jam"...
>
> In the day-time, we tried to walk around on the mountainside, but no sooner would I attempt to ascend the slightest slope, than I would jam like Catherine's Fiat, and I would be compelled to climb down again. I jammed in my anguish beyond all power of description. I jammed in the motions of my body.
>
> I realized that my anguish— my mind, if you prefer— was painfully trying to unite itself with my body; my mind could no longer manifest itself without producing an immediate effect on my body— on matter. Later that action was to exercise itself upon other objects. I seriously set to analyze that vertigo: *my body no longer obeyed the formulas established in my mind, the formulas of old, limited Reason; my will was no longer geared with my faculties of motion; since it no longer possessed any power, it was necessary first of all to liquidate the anguish by which I was paralyzed, then to seek an accord between the mountain, my mind, and my body.* In order to be able to move around in that new world, I had recourse to my heritage of British diplomacy and set aside the strength of my will, seeking, through gentleness, an understanding between the mountain, my body, and my mind.
>
> One day, I went to the mountain alone. At first I could not climb; I lay flat on my face on the slope with the sensation that I was being completely absorbed by the physical sensation of walking with tremendous efforts in some matter as thick as mud. Gradually however,

perceptibly and visibly, it all became easier, and in a few days I was able to negotiate jumps. I could climb vertical walls as easily as any goat. I very seldom got hurt, and *I realized the possibility of a very subtle understanding* which I had not perceived before. Finally, I managed to take no false steps and to wander around easily among the rocks. [Emphasis mine.]

Carrington's actions, at first tentative and simple, revive the intelligence of her body and an ancient association with the earth. She has broken through her social body to reach a source of energy in the physical body that has not yet been shaped by reason or society. Carrington has entered the world of sensation open to the body which reason has tried to close off, by ordering the senses into discrete categories or by ignoring their presentation of truths about reality. This attitude gives Carrington tremendous clarity and power, making her, in the eyes of society, a dangerous woman because she sees through surface conventions into the meanings they are meant to contain and control. Carrington, however, does not sense herself as dangerous; she rejoices in this understanding.

I worshipped myself because I saw myself complete— I was all, all was in me; I rejoiced at seeing my eyes miraculously become a solar system, kindled by their own light, *my motions, a vast and free dance, in which everything was mirrored by every gesture in a limpid and faithful dance...* [Emphasis mine.]

Her dance is abruptly interrupted when she transforms these revelations into a political theory about the war which she presents to the Consul of the British Embassy. In this passage from private to public, from microscopic to macroscopic, Carrington suffers from the momentum of her lucidity as she moves into a political dimension which is not prepared to accept or consider her construction of reality and would rather destroy her than question its own assumptions. Her disturbance of reality is labelled as madness and, as a consequence, she loses her freedom of movement. Initially locked into her hotel room, she is later transported to a clinic, where she is "treated" with injections of Cardiazol.

The fight for her mind directly involves control of her body, and Carrington's descriptions no longer include vast and free dances. Her hands and feet are bound by leather straps and she describes the effects of Cardiazol injections as "absence of motion, fixation, horrible reality." On the one hand, her motion is set against the absence of motion she perceives in the world. She clearly sees her task as setting the world in motion while the world resists her attempts by fixing her position in enforced immobility. Both the physical and spiritual dimensions of her knowledge are metaphorically and literally constrained by the agents of reason, who refuse to consider her views seriously because they threaten to undermine their own structures of sanity, reason, and social purpose. She defines the limit of their reason which they will not transgress and to which they are willing to sacrifice her health. They would rather cross out her vision than cross into the motion she represents.

In an effort to heal herself, Carrington, wrapped in her bed sheet, performs dances in the sun room of the clinic to resolve what she sees as an essential problem between her ego and the male symbol of the sun. She conceptualizes herself as the moon and a woman who carries the knowledge of the earth which must be reinserted into the cosmic order to offset the desiccated knowledge perpetuated by the womanless trinity of god, the son, and the holy ghost. In her state of anguish, clearly lived and resolved through the body, Carrington steps into the symbolic dimension of the ancient female where she knows the lived body as conscious connective tissue between several worlds, including the animal and plant worlds. While the doctors strain to keep her body within the bounds of clinical reason, Carrington gives herself over to private dances meant to concretize her internal designs and stimulate the circulation of much needed female energy in the universe.

In *Women and Madness*, Phyllis Chesler defines madness as "either the acting out of the devalued female role or the total or partial rejection of one's sex-role stereotype." Though this definition may apply to the madness experienced by many women, it does not apply to Carrington, whose state manifests a flight *into* femininity rather than a flight *from* femininity. Not surprisingly, this movement toward the female is equally judged as insane by virtue of its contrariness. Without romanticizing Carrington's state or diminishing her anguish, I think it fair to say she begins to tell the story of women who strip their nerves of the law of the father to receive the maternal ancestry buried by history. In Carrington's case, incarceration taught her two things about this process:

> ... the importance of health, I mean of the absolute necessity of having a healthy body to avoid disaster in the liberation of the mind. More important yet, the necessity that others be with me that we may feed each other with our knowledge and thus constitute the Whole.

In Nazi Europe and Santander, Carrington had neither health nor a community to act with, yet it is obvious from her later involvement in the women's movement and her absolute commitment to the political and cultural evolution of women that she intuited and remembered two key lessons learned under terribly lonely and dangerous circumstances.

Leonora Carrington is eventually released from the insane asylum, quite suddenly discarding her costume of bed sheets and other ritualized objects. She is a woman who "lost" her mind and is now cured. Or is it that she permanently shifted the territory of reason mapped on her body, and learned to protect this new found land from judgements of insanity? Apart from necessities of health and solidarity, Carrington speaks also of having to acquire the ability to "put on and to take off at will the mask which will be my shield against the hostility of Conformism." Is this the function of her art, which carries the imprint of the revelations she writes of in *Down Below*, and more generally, is this the function of art in patriarchy?

One of the major principles of patriarchy is the division of experience into discrete categories including the mind/body division. The body, suppressed by political reasoning, is allowed a limited expression in a category called art which functions as the controlled and political representation of the body. Carrington, I believe, moved below this internalized displacement of the body to realize the possibility of subtle connections at the level of the body. This knowledge could not safely be inserted in the public world except through the agency of art.

Gloria Orenstein has written extensively about the goddess imagery in Carrington's paintings and writings. What is also interesting is the energy embodied in the use of these images and the way in which the painted surface is imbued with motion. In Carrington's paintings, worlds multiply on each other and there is always a world beside the seen world, full of motion and mysterious energies that move in criss-crossing patterns. These paintings are windows multiplying visions into worlds which co-exist with each other, and manifest the energy of the body which Carrington intuited during her stay down below.

2. ZELDA FITZGERALD: ORDER AND DISORDER

At the age of twenty-seven, Zelda Fitzgerald decided to become a professional ballet dancer. This decision was precipitated by a crisis in her marriage to the writer F. Scott Fitzgerald, and it marked the beginning of a difficult transition in her life. Until this time Zelda had cultivated her role as the daring and mischievous wife of her equally daring and mischievous husband. When she finally abandoned her "pink and helpless" role, she turned to dance, which brought her into a world of women and work which she had previously scorned.

Zelda Fitzgerald's search for self and independence is tied, both literally and symbolically, to dance, where her psychical struggles can be tangibly read. Dance gave Zelda the strength to overcome habits of dependency and dissipation and it answered her need to make something of her own from life. Though she never became a "great" dancer and she accepted this as a bitter and sorrowful defeat, her relation with dance is deeply moving and shows how building a relation with the self through the body is a way of acknowledging and entering the powers of the self.

Zelda Sayre was born in 1900 in Montgomery, Alabama. In 1920, she married Fitzgerald, who had just published his first successful book, *This Side of Paradise*. Zelda was apparently content to live by her husband's ambition until 1927, when an extra-marital affair and an attempted suicide led her to become a professional ballet dancer. After a year of intense physical work, Zelda became ill. Her breakdown was the first in a series which eventually led to her permanent institutionalization. Zelda's very real illness cannot be separated from her prodigious talent, expressed through dancing, writing, and painting. Nor can it be separated from the conflicts faced by the female artist in patriarchal culture.

The decision to become a dancer freed Zelda into her own life in a terrifying way which she met with a single-minded determination to work. This dedication to work meant a radical change in her everyday life. In a letter to her husband Scott, Zelda writes about the meaning this work had come to take in her life:

> I had to work because I couldn't exist in the world without it, still I didn't understand what I was doing. I didn't even know what I wanted.

The letter from which this excerpt is taken, written in 1930 from the Prangins Clinic in Nyon, Switzerland, where she was being treated for a breakdown, sums up Zelda's view of her life with Scott from the early days of their marriage through to the onset of her illness. The beginning of the letter is rich in excitement and happiness, as Zelda rushes from event to event in a catalogue of impulsive episodes, wild parties, and reckless pranks described in staccato sentences. Somewhere between Paris and New York, she and Scott both lose control. The crack-up, Zelda believes, is caused by Scott's drinking, and she explains how she took up dance as a way of confronting the emptiness that materialized:

You were constantly drunk. You didn't work and were dragged home at night by taxi-drivers when you came home at all. You said it was my fault for dancing all day. What was I to do?

Through dance, she begins to claim her own identity as an artist, moving into difficult and uncertain places of power and creativity and confronting a sense of inertia which she claims "hovers over my life and everything I do."

In taking on the work of becoming a dancer Zelda made a commitment to developing her internal resources and to working for an ideal whose value was not determined by male approval. For the first time ever she was taking on the subject of her life in a conscious, directed way, that differed radically from the perception she had held of herself as the model flapper of the jazz age. In two articles, published in 1922 and 1925, Zelda writes a description of the flapper, outlining the flapper's creed and her own philosophy of life before her commitment to dance became central. Both of these articles were commissioned as slick celebrity pieces from the young wife of a famous writer and they provide a limited view of Zelda Fitzgerald's private world. One thing, however, is clear: they emphasize her identification with the personality of the flapper and they outline the work that lay ahead in her struggles to become an artist:

I believe in the flapper as an involuntary and invaluable cup-bearer to the arts. I believe in the flapper as an artist in her particular field, the art of being— being young, being lovely, being an object.

For almost the first time we are developing a class of pretty yet respectable young women, whose sole functions are to amuse and to make growing old a more enjoyable process for some men and staying young an easier one for others.

In Zelda's articles on the flapper, three characteristics stand out: the flapper is an object, she is male-identified, and she has tremendous vitality. Like the goddess Athene/Minerva, the flapper is born complete from her father's head and her primary identification is with men, beginning with the father, "upon whom she lavishes affection and reverence, and deepest filial regard." She has no mother and no meaningful relation with women. Very baldly, Zelda lets us know that the flapper had "mostly masculine friends."

Not surprisingly, the flapper's relation to her body is completely determined by appearance and the effect she will have upon men. Her relation to the body is mediated by make-up and clothes, and though she is endowed with great vitality, it is meant only to attract men and make her the centre of attention. Unlike the dancer, the flapper has no physical power— she is pure appearance— and the words Zelda uses to describe her are very different from the words she later uses to describe the dancer.

In her essay "Why Have There Been No Great Women Artists?" Linda Nochlin identifies the characteristics needed by a successful woman artist:

> ... for a woman to opt for a career at all, much less for a career in art, has required a certain amount of unconventionality, both in the past and at present; whether or not the woman artist rebels against or finds strength in the attitude of her family, she must in any case have a good strong streak of rebellion in her to make her way in the world of art at all, rather than submitting to the socially approved role of wife and mother, the only role to which every social institution consigns her automatically. It is only by adopting, however covertly, the "masculine" attributes of single-mindedness, concentration, tenaciousness, and absorption in ideas and craftsmanship for their own sake, that women have succeeded, and continue to succeed, in the world of art.

Except for rebelliousness, none of the qualities Nochlin defines as necessary for the woman artist match with the characteristics Zelda attributes to the flapper and to herself. On the contrary, it is painfully obvious in her struggle to define herself first as a dancer, then as a writer, that her first enemy was the flapper she had once admired. Zelda had prided herself on an unconventional and rebellious attitude which had endeared her to Scott's friends and admirers, but this behaviour is different from the unconventionality Nochlin describes. Without discipline or craft to give substance to rebelliousness, Zelda's behaviour manifested itself in destructive acts of drinking and socializing which gave her no lasting satisfaction.

Zelda had no work to support or protect her, and until her life with Scott began to disintegrate in an endless round of drinking and empty socializing, she shunned the idea of a career, though she once remarked in a mock interview with Scott that if she ever had to support herself she would become a dancer. In the transition from being a cup-bearer of the arts to doing the work of an artist, Zelda's life changed completely: her marriage to Scott dissolved, she was separated from her beloved daughter, and she endured a series of hospital treatments and periodic stays in asylums until she committed herself permanently to Highland Hospital in Asheville, North Carolina. Foremost among these changes was her changing relation to women. When Zelda accepted the need to change in herself her relation to other women also shifted. Dance provided her with meaningful work and companionship with women which she had never experienced. It gave her the chance to see women artists at work, living by the kind of tenaciousness and single-minded concentration characteristic of artists, which she had previously witnessed only in male artists. In a recapitulation of her life with Scott she lists their friends and acquaintances, all male. Her comment on this sexual breakdown of friends is consistent with the philosophy of the flapper who did not acknowledge female companionship or solidarity. "We did not like women and we were happy," she writes.

This is in contrast to another letter written to Scott during her first stay in an asylum. In this letter, she writes about her feelings for Madame Lubov Egorova, her ballet mistress in Paris: "My attitude to Egorova has always been one of an intense love." Clearly, Zelda is conflicted about this love, for she also writes that, "... it was wrong, of course, to love my teacher when I should have loved you. But I didn't have you to love— not since long before I loved her."

In Egorova, Zelda had found a role model and someone to encourage her ambition to become a professional ballet dancer. Egorova believed in Zelda's talent and taught her on a daily basis how discipline and order relate to artistic achievement. In a letter to Scott, Zelda remembers how her ballet mistress "helped me to learn more, to go further. She always told me to look after myself. I tried to... " In Zelda's eyes, Egorova had successfully managed a life as a dancer and choreographer. The beauty and grace Egorova personified and her willingness to teach Zelda the means to achieve this beauty allowed Zelda to believe that she also might participate in a larger transcendent order if she worked hard enough. For the first time, Zelda had before her the role model of a successful woman artist and someone who demanded that she work with discipline and order toward a goal. Egorova asked that Zelda literally stretch herself, giving Zelda the strength to believe that she also was capable of a higher level of achievement and that she could successfully solve the conflicts raging in and around her.

Dance is a highly disciplined art form which asks that the dancer's whole life be devoted in a very intimate way to her work in the studio. Specifically, a dancer has to be careful of what she eats and drinks; she has to regulate her sleeping habits and live a regular life to be productive in her daily practising. Until her commitment to dance, Zelda's life had been anything but orderly, and she fought very hard to create the external order she needed to work.

The regularity Zelda needed to impose on her life for the sake of dance conflicted with the life she had achieved with Scott. In her description of her initial commitment to dance, Zelda speaks of Scott's increasingly dishevelled life— he drinks, stays up all night, and doesn't work— while she attempts to lead a highly disciplined life, abstaining from late nights and alcohol and working obsessively all day. There is a bitterness evident in both of their writings about this time. Zelda writes:

I began to work harder at dancing. I thought of nothing else but that. You were far away by then and I was alone...

You wouldn't help me— I don't blame you by now, but if you had explained I would have understood because all I wanted was to go on working. You had other things: drink and tennis, and we did not care about each other.

For his part, Scott feels more and more abandoned by Zelda, as he explains to her doctor:

After having worked all day at home, I would want to go out at night— my wife, on the contrary, having been gone all day, wanted only to stay home and go to bed... The last six months she did not even take any interest in our child... Before she devoted herself to the ballet she took care of all her duties and more.

And later:

The ballet idea was something I inaugurated in 1927 to stop her idle drinking after she had already so lost herself in it as to make suicidal attempts. Since then I have drunk more, from unhappiness, and she less, because of her physical work...

Dance gave order to Zelda's life, allowing her to cut back on alcohol and face her dependency on Scott, but it also created tremendous pressure. While she was studying dance, Zelda tried daily to come to grips with her own identity and her ability to create something of substance apart from her relation with Scott. Dance became a way for her to have a life of her own, and the studio a private place where she could work out her damaging dependencies. Zelda's recognition of her need to work was also the recognition of a talent and ambition which had been subsumed under the role of wife and support to Scott's ambition. Until Zelda chose to work, she and Scott assumed that his work alone was of value. This assumption culminated in an illness which her doctor classified as a "reaction to her feelings of inferiority (primarily toward her husband)." Clearly, her breakdown was the result of years of accumulated frustration in which she had repressed or dissipated her talent.

With the urgency to work exacerbated by age, Zelda toiled obsessively to make up for lost time in a profession where age mattered. As a child, she had taken ballet lessons, and according to the local paper had shown some promise. In 1916, at the age of fifteen, she had appeared in a ballet recital that had launched her popularity as a belle in her home town of Asheville. The local paper reported that, "She might dance like Pavlova if her nimble feet were not so busy keeping up with the pace of a string of young but ardent admirers set before her." Zelda quickly gave up these ballet lessons to devote herself to cultivating the "ardent admirers," and later in life she reversed this decision, returning to this first blush of success to retrieve her identity by working through the body.

According to friends and family, Zelda worked furiously, practising intensively every day. She aspired to a professional position with a company, and Ergorova believed her capable of this achievement. Whether or not Zelda was capable of achieving professional status is a question which obscures her deepest needs with regard to dance. Clearly she wanted to achieve professional status as a way of marking her progress and measuring her ability against Scott's professional achievements. But beneath this need was the greater need to express and direct the energy that till then had only created chaos in her life.

The physical order Zelda learned through ballet was mirrored internally in her psychic development. During the hours of repeating her ballet steps, Zelda was literally reinventing herself. During her ballet lessons and private sessions she was circling back to a former child self who had known tremendous vitality and confidence:

When I was a little girl, I had great confidence in myself, even to the extent of walking by myself against life as it was then. I did not have a single feeling of inferiority, or shyness, or doubt, and no moral principles.

The transition from ambitious, courageous child to a young woman consumed with doubt and inferiority, "hideously dependent" on her husband, is a classic example of the change which occurs in young girls as they become aware of conventional female roles. Zelda was encouraged to concentrate on domestic happiness, and when this threatened her ability to survive, she hoped that the work of dance would enable her to reverse the inertia which had taken the place of her previous vitality.

Zelda's work in dance is full of conflict between two qualities best summarized by what Adrienne Rich has called the "energy of creation" and the "energy of relation." The energy of creation represents ambition, talent, individual power, and the need to create a transcendent relation with others through work. The "energy of relation" represents the need for love, companionship, family, and the need to create private relations of growth with others. This larger conflict is played out in a host of other conflicts: the conflict between her acquired inertia and the discipline required to produce meaningful work, the conflict between her feelings of inferiority and the confidence needed to generate meaningful work, the conflict between her ambition and her husband's ambition, the conflict between the artistic measure of her ability and the actualization of her talent, the conflict between the order needed for work and the disorder which characterized her life.

All of these conflicts were exacerbated by Scott's evaluation of Zelda's work and his belief that she would never achieve professional status. Scott's opinions of Zelda's abilities as a dancer are not objective.

Even though he supported her materially for the rest of his life, he never came to terms with his wife's ambitions to dance. And when she made clear her intention to write, he became overtly hostile.

Dance provided Zelda with the physical and emotional strength she needed to begin the work of putting herself together, slowly shaping the body and mind to act together for a common purpose and literally creating a space for herself in her everyday family life. Unlocking this physical and emotional energy also freed Zelda's imagination, and she began to write: six stories, some written with Scott's help, others written by herself. Practically, dance was at the core of her writing, which she hoped would provide her with money to pay for her dance classes. "I hated taking his money for my lessons: I wanted my dancing to belong to me, so I wrote to pay for them." Artistically, dance provided her with a theme for her first novel, *Save Me the Waltz*, written after she had given up dancing.

Much as she needed dance for her well-being, Zelda's commitment was always fragile. Dancing exhausted her. Her involvement in it was not sufficient to undo the habits of dependency and frivolity instilled in childhood, the inferiority reinforced in her marriage to Scott, his ongoing resentment of her ambition, and her own insecurities about her ability to become an artist. With virtually no support, she continued to struggle. In a sense, dance tricked and failed her. She had hoped that it could lead her into a life of happiness, rest, and work, but it alone could not overcome all the contradictions of being female and being an artist.

Dance did provide some relief from these contradictions, and it continued to so do even after she had formally given it up. When at home, she would lock herself in a room and dance for herself; in the clinics, dancing and exercise classes tempered her hostility. She composed ballets about herself and Scott, once performing a fragment at a costume ball; she taught an exercise class during one of her stays at Highland Hospital. And, like de Beauvoir, she walked five miles a day, a habit acquired during her treatment at Highland that continued to the end of her life.

Through dance and her body, Zelda had formulated an image of perfection and beauty necessary for her life. "The only message I ever thought I had was four pirouettes and a fouetté. It turned out to be about as cryptic a one as [a] Chinese laundry ticket, but the will to speak remains." What was most important about her commitment to dance was that she finally recovered this "will to speak" and she worked to give it a form outside of herself, engaging in shared work with her teacher and other dancers in the studio. Sharing this work enlarged Zelda's world and relieved the isolation she felt in her life with Scott. Supported by the order dance imposes, she was able to turn away from self-destruction and initiate a process of self-creation.

Writing also plays a part in Zelda's renewed commitment to herself. In daring to claim the territory of language which Scott had already staked as his own, Zelda directly confronted her feelings of inferiority and her dependency on Scott. Before she began to publish under her own name, Scott had already used some of Zelda's writing in his own work. In a review of *The Beautiful and the Damned*, Zelda writes,

> It seems to me that on one page I recognized a portion of an old diary of mine which mysteriously disappeared shortly after my marriage, and also scraps of letters which, though considerably edited, sound to me vaguely familiar. In fact, Mr. Fitzgerald— I believe that is how he spells his name— seems to believe that plagiarism begins at home.

This accusation, though playfully tossed, foreshadows Zelda's later attempt to retrieve the material of her life, both in actual fact and on the written page. Writing was not a neutral ground for Zelda or for Scott, and it became a place of struggle between them, as Scott claimed his place as the only writer in their family. Zelda, writing from the asylums and clinics, tried to recover and give form to her will to speak. Her ambition to become a professional dancer confused and threatened their marital relation; her ambition to write confused and threatened his artistic identity. Angrily, he accused her of stealing his material, of being a second-rate writer, and of exploiting her relation to him. Though deeply pained by these accusations, Zelda continued to write, sustaining a fragile belief in her talent and her right to create an artistic identity and product from her experience. Her tenacity on this tender issue is a measure of how critical the achievement of independence was for her, and of how she needed to separate her life from Scott's to recognize the value in her own ambitions and desire.

In *Save Me the Waltz*, Zelda articulates a philosophy of the body founded on her experience with dance. The novel is about questioning the body of the father/husband and, through the establishment of a relation with dance and other women, pushing at the limits of the daughter/wife body. The issues Zelda addresses in *Save Me the Waltz* resonate with the issues she addressed in her own life and the difficulties she faced in her attempt to reinvent an artistic identity.

In *Save Me the Waltz*, Zelda maps her struggles to become a professional ballet dancer onto the main character, Alabama Beggs. Writing with the freedom that fiction gives, Zelda reflects in a more self-conscious way on the importance of the body in the achievement of autonomy and self-identity. Like Zelda, Alabama was raised in the South in a family where the father, Judge Beggs, holds a classical patriarchal position. As a judge, he maintains a powerful and well-respected position in his community. At home, he is head of the household and the representative of logic and reason in the life of his wife Millie and his three daughters, Dixie, Joan, and Alabama. The paternal figure is the reference point in the Beggs household; the maternal figure operates entirely within the parameters of the masculine tradition, where she represents emotional anarchy and the powerless underside of patriarchal logic. "Alabama's father was a wise man. Alone his preference in women had created Millie and the girls. He knew everything she said to herself." Alabama is cast in the role of the classical daughter who identifies with the desires of the benevolent father and his regulation of every aspect of her life. Respectful and obedient, she is not encouraged to develop her own will or to act according to her own desires. On the contrary, her role is to fit her father's perception of her, and when the time comes, to transfer this role to her husband, who will become the new directive force in her life.

Alabama learns this dynamic very early on as she observes her older sister Joan with an unwelcome boyfriend:

> Alabama watched them enviously as Harlan held Joey's coat and took her off possessively. Speculatively she watched her sister change into a more fluctuating, more ingratiating person, as she confided herself to the man. She wished it were herself. There would be her father at the supper table. It was nearly the same; the necessity of being something that you really weren't was the same. Her father didn't know what she really was like, she thought.

Alabama's upbringing does not prepare her to identify her desires and to make decisions for herself. Consequently, by the time Alabama meets the painter, David Knight, who will become her husband, she has a vague sense of her real identity. David, on the other hand, has a clearly defined identity derived from his work as a painter. The contrast between her confused identity and his clear direction is expressed in a game with their names.

> "David," the legend read, "David, David, Knight, Knight, Knight, and Miss Alabama Nobody."
> "Egotist," she protested... She was a little angry about the names. David had told her about how famous he was going to be many times before.

Just as she had followed the boundaries set by the Judge, Alabama willingly accepts the direction David sets for their life. However, as soon as trouble occurs between them, she blames David for the dissatisfaction in her life in the same way that she had blamed her father for holding her back from her childhood and adolescent desires.

When she was a child and the days slipped lazily past in the same indolent fashion, she had not thought of life as furnishing up the slow uneventful sequence, but of the Judge as meting it out that way, curtailing the excitement she considered was her due. She began to blame David for the monotony.

In abdicating the power of her life, first to the Judge, then to her husband, Alabama ended up confusing life itself with her father's and then her husband's will. As intermediaries between herself and life, Alabama held them responsible for her happiness and her unhappiness, not thinking that she herself might take on this responsibility or that it properly belonged with her. Her upbringing encouraged this abdication to paternal power, and it was only when she entered the maternal territory of the body through dance that she began to understand and act on her responsibilities to herself.

Alabama reaches the decision to become a ballet dancer on the night her husband begins an extra-marital affair. The symbolic end of her marriage marks a transition into her own life: on the same night that David's affair releases her, dance claims her. For the first time, Alabama confronts her lack of accomplishment and she commits herself to working for something of her own. It is a revolutionary moment in her life, though she is not fully aware of its importance and of where this engagement will take her. While watching a performance of the Russian ballet, she resolves to take lessons. Her description of the event reads almost like a religious conversion or a moment of revelation:

The decor swarmed in Saturnian rings. Spare, immaculate legs and a consciousness of rib, the vibrant suspension of lean bodies precipitated on the jolt of reiterant rhythmic shock, the violins' hysteria, evolved themselves to a tortured abstraction of sex. Alabama's excitement rose with the appeal to the poignancy of a human body subject to its physical will to the point of evangelism. Her hands were wet and shaking with its tremolo. Her heart beat like the fluttering wings of an angry bird.

In the ballet movements, Alabama recognizes the exuberance and freedom she had enjoyed as a child. At the same time, when she begins her lessons, she resents her body and its resistance to the movements the ballet mistress demands of her. Yet her body's resistance and Madame's prodding only strengthen her resolve to work. The ballet has opened up a world for her and provided her with the possibility of giving order to her internal confusion. Dance, she thinks, might be able to save her from the unhappiness she has known:

> At night she sat in the window too tired to move, consumed by a longing to succeed as a dancer. It seemed to Alabama that, reaching her goal, she would drive out the devils that had driven her— that, in proving herself, she would achieve that peace which she imagined went only in surety of one's self— that she would be able, through the medium of the dance, to command her emotions, to summon love or pity or happiness at will, having provided a channel through which they might flow.

Alabama finds her work in the company of women, with the ballet mistress and the dancers in the studio. Her world, which had been almost exclusively defined by men and pleasure, is now almost exclusively defined by women and work.

With the support of her fellow dancers and with Madame's example, Alabama begins to grow into her own life, taking responsibility for her successes and failures. In Alabama's studio experience, Zelda Fitzgerald gives us the picture of women with common interests and values. The women still quarrel with each other over husbands, money, and clothes, and she once refers to their behaviour as typical of squabbling fishwives. Yet, overall, Zelda Fitzgerald conveys a sense of companionship and sisterly affection as well as a feeling of friendly competition as they push themselves to achieve.

At home, David remains doubtful of Alabama's ambition and her ability to achieve professional status. Like Scott, upon whom he is modeled, David cannot reconcile his wife with his image of a professional artist.

> "You're so thin," said David patronizingly. "There's no use killing yourself. I hope that you realize that the biggest difference in the world is between the amateur and the professional in the arts."
>
> "You might mean yourself and me— " she said thoughtfully.

When Alabama is offered a professional role, David invokes familial duties and a trip to America, promising that they will arrange a perform-ance for her in America. In a momentary flash of insight, Alabama realizes the emptiness of his promise and she grasps at her work. Impulsively, she asks Madame to confirm her appearance in Naples, and she promises to leave the following day, despite her husband's objections and the pull of familial obligations. It is a conscious act of rebellion against David's judgement of her "amateur" status, and a moment of affirmation for the professional level she has achieved. For Alabama, there is no joy in this moment of achievement; it is read only as another moment in the continuing struggle between herself and David, between her family life, domestic happiness, and her career. Even in this moment of success, the two poles of her life remain separate. Success does not resolve the conflicts she has encountered, nor does it mediate the gap between the different parts of her life.

In her decision to go to Naples, Alabama chooses to affirm her career as a professional ballet dancer. She tries to communicate the value of this choice to her daughter, Bonnie, against her husband's will, who complains that one ballet dancer in the family is enough. Since dance showed her the way into her own life, Alabama takes Bonnie to Madame for dance lessons, hoping that her little girl will learn early on the value of work and bypass the adult struggles she has known. In actual life, Zelda had herself revised the prescription for happiness for her own daughter. When her daughter, Scottie, was born, Zelda wished her beauty and wealth; later, she wished her the acquisition of meaningful work. In the novel, when Bonnie visits her mother in Naples, she declares that she will be rich and her mother admonishes her: "You will have to work to get what you want— that's why I wanted you to dance," she says to the child. By this time, Bonnie has given up dance, but her mother continues to instill in her the value of work. In a touching way, she tries to protect her child from the emptiness she had known in her own life and she tries to give her child the tools to become autonomous and free. When Bonnie returns to France to her father, she repeats the advice of her mother, puzzled by its meaning:

> "She said— let me see— I don't know what Mummy said, Daddy, only she said her piece of advice that she had to give me was not to be a backseat driver about life."
> "Did you understand?"
> "Oh, no," sighed Bonnie gratefully and complacently.

In the novel, a physical, not a mental illness prevents Alabama from continuing her dance career. Crippled by a foot infection which almost claims her life, Alabama is forced to give up dance after a modest success in an Italian company in Naples where she had been promised a leading role. On leaving the hospital, Alabama returns to America to be with her dying father. At his deathbed, she reflects on her belief that the body could reveal a secret formula for a full, satisfying life. At this point, she is still looking to the body of the father for an answer, not yet realizing or fully accepting that she is herself the answer and instrument of her life and that her own body can be trusted to bring her to the truth she needs for her life. Not surprisingly, the body of the father who has limited her desires and her existence fails her.

> "I thought you could tell me if our bodies are given to us as counter-irritants to the soul. I thought you'd know why when our bodies ought to bring surcease from our tortured minds, they fail and collapse; and why, when we are tormented in our bodies, does our soul desert us as a refuge?"
> The old man lay silent.
> "Why do we spend years using up our bodies to nurture our minds with experience and find our minds turning then to our exhausted bodies for solace? Why, Daddy?"
> "Ask me something easy," the old man answered, very weak and far away.

In the end, Alabama does not receive an answer from her father, and her passion for dance is absorbed into David's paintings. She brings up the image of herself as goddess, remembering how her father had said to her:

> "If you want to choose, you must be a goddess." That was when she had wanted her own way about things. It wasn't easy to be a goddess away from Olympus.

Unable to claim the maternal territory fully and to take pride and satisfaction in being her own goddess, Alabama refers her power back to the male Olympus, thereby locking herself out of the truth and power of her own existence.

Alabama and Zelda, whom she represents, never fully aligned themselves with the maternal power of the body, though dance gave them the freedom and discipline to work through in the company of women the limitations in their bones. After leaving dance, Zelda lived out her life in an asylum, where she continued to work with her body in different ways, painting and choreographing, no longer concerned with professional achievement. Dance, which had clarified so much for her, continued to inform her life:

> What I want to do is to paint the basic, fundamental principle so that everyone will be forced to realize and experience it— I want to paint a ballet step so all will know what it is...

3. H.D.: WOMAN IS PERFECT

In the work of the poet H.D., the writer and woman artist is completely identified with the dancer. The image of the dancer is not an accidental choice of poetic metaphor but the result of a deep and powerful shift in consciousness documented in H.D.'s poems, novels, essays, and autobiographical writings. This shift from an abstract consciousness of the mind to a more integrated body consciousness occurs over a period of several years and is highlighted by three significant events. The first of these occurred in 1919 in the Scilly Islands, in what H.D. came to call the bell-jar experience. The second occurred a year later in Corfu, and came to be known as the writing-on-the-wall episode. The third occurred in Vienna in 1933, when H.D. undertook an analysis of these experiences with Freud. I believe that the bell-jar experience, the writing-on-the-wall episode, and the Freudian analysis all lead to a greater awareness of a maternal consciousness which H.D. eventually resolved in the poetic image of the dancer. H.D. traced the evolution of this consciousness in four texts: the essays *Notes on Thought and Vision* and *Tribute to Freud*, and the poems "The Master" and "The Dancer."

H.D. first experiences this maternal consciousness during a trip to the Scilly Islands in 1919. The circumstances leading up to the trip indicate that, at the time, she was in a state of mental collapse brought about by the war, which had deeply affected her, and by difficulties in her private life. H.D. had just given birth to her daughter after a dangerous pregnancy and delivery. Her husband, recently returned from the war, abandoned her upon discovering that the child was not his; he further threatened her with imprisonment to prevent her from giving the child his name. The war, her shattered relationship, the illness, and her responsibility for a newborn all contributed to H.D.'s breakdown. She was saved by a woman, Bryher, who was to become her lifelong companion and protector. Bryher was with H.D. during both the bell-jar experience and the writing-on-the-wall episode.

H.D. describes the bell-jar experience and Bryher's part in it in *Advent,* written in 1933:

> We were in the little room that Bryher had taken for our study when I felt this impulse to "let go" into a sort of balloon, or diving-bell, as I have explained it, that seemed to hover over me... There was, I explained to Bryher, a second globe or bell-jar rising as if it were from my feet. I was enclosed. I felt I was safe but seeing things as through water. I felt the double globe come and go and I could have dismissed it at once and probably would have if I had been alone. But it would not have happened, I imagine, if I had been alone. It was being with Bryher that projected the fantasy...

In a more immediate attempt to record the bell-jar experience, H.D. wrote a short essay entitled *Notes on Thought and Vision* which contains the seed of an idea about the body she later developed in her poetry. In *Notes,* H.D. is trying to integrate the body and mind, to overcome the dualistic split of body and mind. In her attempt to heal this break, she gropes for words, clumsily trying to conjure a vision of wholeness which she achieves much later with poetic grace in "The Master" and "The Dancer," poems where the image of the dancer emerges to convey the wholeness of body and mind H.D. was just beginning to sense. Guest interprets H.D.'s bell-jar experience as a breakdown, which it surely was, but like Carrington's breakdown, it precedes a shift in consciousness toward a more physical way of thinking and creating.

H.D. first realizes this state of consciousness in her head and later visualizes it in the womb. She uses the metaphor of the jelly-fish to describe this consciousness as feelers of thought extending into her body. H.D. is clearly experimenting with consciousness and states of mind and is able to do so for two reasons. First, she is in a weakened and vulnerable state; second, she has the assurance of Bryher's presence to pull her back to safety if necessary. In her description of the experience, H.D. locates the sensations in the body.

Vision is of two kinds— vision of the womb and vision of the brain. In vision of the brain, the region of consciousness is above and about the head; when the centre of consciousness shifts and the jelly-fish is in the body, (I visualize it in my case lying on the left side with the streamers of feelers floating up toward the brain) we have vision of the womb or love-vision.

The majority of dream and of ordinary vision is vision of the womb.

The brain and the womb are both centres of consciousness, equally important.

Notes is about the body and about the ways in which thinking through the body is possible. H.D. roots this awareness in the experience of birthing her daughter, which brought the "jelly-fish consciousness" to her conscious attention. Though she is missing a convincing language, H.D. probes the body for the sense of this awareness. Later she will develop a language and images to take her further into the consciousness of the body. Meanwhile, like the character in Zelda Fitzgerald's novel, she asks, "Where does the body come in? What is the body?", only turning inward for the answer, not to a dying patriarch.

H.D.'s second experience with this consciousness occurs a year later on the Greek island of Corfu. Again, she is accompanied by Bryher, who provides the context in which she can explore this new way of thinking. Bryher's role as attendant was essential to H.D.'s vision. In any initiation ritual, attendants are needed to watch over the initiates, to guard against harm and to take them safely through the ritual. In a very real sense, the relation between H.D. and Bryher was the enactment of an old and sacred ritual bond between women.

> And yet, so oddly, I knew that this experience, this writing-on-the-wall before me... could not be shared with anyone except the girl who stood so bravely there beside me. This girl had said without hesitation, "Go on." It was she really who had the detachment and the integrity of the Pythoness of Delphi. But it was I, battered and disassociated from my American family and my English friends, who was seeing the pictures, who was reading the writing or who was granted the inner vision. Or perhaps in some sense, we were "seeing" it together, for without her, admittedly, I could not have gone on.

This time the consciousness manifests itself externally, in a series of pictures on the wall of her hotel room. Initially H.D. had simply thought the images were shadows being cast on the wall, but she soon realized that the pictures were made up of light on shadow and not shadow on light. Her head, she says, warned her that she was in an "unusual dimension" and experiencing an unusual way of thinking. Urged on by Bryher, she overcomes her hesitation and concentrates on deciphering the images: the head and shoulders of a soldier or airman, the outline of a goblet or cup, a three-dimensional design of circles and lines, a tripod with tiny people buzzing at its base, a ladder of light, a figure of a woman or a goddess moving up the ladder, and a series of question marks. The very last image is deciphered by Bryher, who is able to see the writing-on-the-wall only after H.D. looks away. The final image is a circle with a male figure in the centre, drawing the woman or goddess toward him with one arm.

On the surface, H.D. translates these visions into symbols drawn directly from Greek and Biblical mythology. The soldier is a dead brother or a lost friend. The goblet represents the mystic chalice. The tripod is a symbol of poetry, prophecy, and hidden knowledge, while the shadow people at its base represent all those who cannot participate in divine knowledge. The ladder is Jacob's ladder and the woman or goddess climbing it is Nike or Victory. The question marks represent all the mysteries and questions that continue to be asked through time. The last image, she speculates, determines the meaning of all the symbols before it. It is clear by itself— a symbolic union of man and woman, or god and goddess, in a sacred circle.

Of the fact of the writing itself, she suggests two possibilities:

> We can read my writing, the fact that there was writing, in two ways or in more than two ways. We can read or translate it as a suppressed desire for forbidden "signs and wonders," breaking bounds, a suppressed desire to be a Prophetess, to be important anyway, megalomania they call it... Or this writing-on-the-wall is merely an extension of the artist's mind, a picture or an illustrated poem, taken out of the actual dream or day-dream content and projected from within (though apparently from outside), really a high-powered idea, simply over-stressed, over-thought, you might say, an echo of an idea, a reflection of a reflection, a "freak" thought that had got out of hand, gone too far, a "dangerous symptom."

But the writing-on-the-wall is more than a dangerous symptom of illness or the sign of exaggerated artistic inspiration; both H.D. and Freud recognize this, as she concentrates intensely to follow the vision and he focuses on its analytic value. Its deep importance lies not so much in the symbolic references as in the fact that they emanate from a different way of sensing and thinking. The importance is in the context that makes such a vision possible and the means of allowing it outward expression. H.D. describes her efforts in terms of drowning and being reborn:

> In a sense, it seems I am drowning; already half-drowned to the ordinary dimensions of space and time, I know that I must drown, as it were, completely in order to come out on the other side of things (like Alice with her looking-glass or Perseus with his mirror). I must drown completely and come out on the other side, or rise to the surface after the third time down, not dead to this life but with a new set of values, my treasure dredged from the depth. I must be born again or break utterly.

It is Freud who finally uncovers the deeper meaning of these experiences: it is, he says, a desire for union with her mother. This desire for union with the mother does not involve simply H.D.'s actual mother. It is the desire to inhabit a maternal consciousness, symbolized both by H.D.'s own mother and by the mother H.D. herself had become. And it is a desire to inhabit the body as the realm of the maternal.

Throughout her work and her life, H.D. presents multiple visions of the mother. There is H.D.'s real mother, Helen, described by H.D. in *The Gift* and *Tribute to Freud*. This mother is painting and music and self-effacing in her power. Thinking in images and sounds, she is pre-verbal, part of a symbolic order that has no power compared to the power of the father and his science. There is H.D. herself, whom her daughter touchingly describes in the afterword to the novel *Hedylus*:

> H.D. was hardly an archetypal mother, nor would one expect her to be... for all I knew, everybody's mother was a poet; a tall figure of striking beauty, with fine bone structure and haunting grey eyes; and frequently overwrought, off in the clouds, or sequestered in a room, not to be disturbed on any account... a mother was someone who wrote poetry and was very nervous. And who walked alone

and sat alone. Who was capable of overwhelming affection, but on her own time and terms preferably out of doors.

In the novel *Hedylus*, H.D.'s second novel, set in classical Greece, there is the mother as mother-goddess, mother-poetry, and work itself. The multiple visions of the mother are projected from and onto the mother in the novel. Hedyle is seen primarily through the eyes of her son, Hedylus, and we catch her in quiet moments reflecting on her son and her voyage away from Athens. Hedyle of Athens has come to the island of Samos, where she lives under the protection of the tyrant Douris. She is "synonymous with Athens," the old Athens of prophetesses, seers, visions, and mystery rites. Living on with the tyrant in a foreign land, she is considered by some to be an "indifferent prostitute," a "queen in hiding," or a "goddess." It is her son Hedylus who identifies her most intimately with poetry and work:

> His poetry remained in his thought, along with his mother, unformulated, vague. Poetry? Hedylus didn't know why his attitude to Hedyle should have crept in. He supposed, facing it frankly, that his work was his secret mother, the mother that answered when he claimed her, that gave him return for caresses, that never grumbled at his belt-clasp.

In the novel, Hedylus replicates for us H.D.'s own conflicting sense of her mother's visionary but powerless self, set against the power she perceived in the tools of her father and his science. Like H.D., Hedylus is a poet, and as a poet he has two lives, or two faces. The one is the public rhyming face, accepted by his peers and the aristocrats of the tyrant's court. The other is the face of poetry, more private and more authentic in Hedylus' view, secret and hidden by the sea. He had, we are told, "for common occasion a separate parchment, open to all eyes" while his real work exists elsewhere. To get to his poetry, to his real work, Hedylus, like H.D., risks drowning and makes a dangerous descent to the sea, where he retrieves the manuscripts of his authentic voice from their hiding place. Reading aloud to the moon and the sea, Hedylus becomes frustrated with the work, judging it worthless and inadequate. At the point where he is ready to abandon the work, a stranger appears. The stranger listens to the poems, and through his appreciation and understanding of the poetry, brings about the desired unity in Hedylus, healing the spiritual cleavage felt by the poet. The man/god/father recognizes the poetry's strongest element— imagery. "Your imagery was excellent," he says, recalling H.D.'s own poetic gift. Like H.D., Hedylus is gifted with strong imagery, and like H.D. his work is validated by a male figure who gives him the confidence needed to risk a more public exposure of his private voice.

In *End to Torment*, H.D. tells how Ezra Pound confidently gave her both her poetic name and identity.

"But Dryad," (in the Museum tea room), "this is poetry." He slashed with a pencil. "Cut this out, shorten this line. 'Hermes of the Ways' is a good title. I'll send this to Harriet Monroe of *Poetry*. Have you a copy? Yes? Then we can send this, or I'll type it when I get back. Will this do?" And he scrawled "H.D. Imagiste" at the bottom of the page.

Hedylus, like H.D., struggles "half with half," sensing in himself a double identity, two selves that do not allow himself to feel whole. This double life is lived in his poetic identity and experienced in relation to his mother Hedyle. Hedyle, we are left to understand, is the mother-poetry, the mother-work of old visionary Athens and, by itself, incomplete until the appearance of the man/god/father. His voice and his perception make whole both the poetry and the poet:

Self met self as two waves, for long chafing at some fragile sand barrier, finally join, white with white crests; irradiating a fine spray that told, in an exact moment, that the tiny demarcation of dividing sand (dividing self) was merged, submerged in one wavelength of silver. Cold. Hedylus recognized the exact moment when the old cleft was healed and each self satisfied.

"It would be banal to presume that you might be my father." The flash answering his smile told him that no claim of mere physical fatherhood could make for such poignancy of understanding.

The stranger also makes whole the mother, who is herself afflicted with a sense of doubleness and foreign identity. As a stranger in Samos and as a representative of old Athens, she never finds her place among the tyrant's people. Isolated and alienated, she feels her own identity as an Athenian slipping away. This identity is returned her when her son decides to leave the island and the stranger, who is a long-lost lover from Athens, visits her. At this moment, H.D. defines the mother as "suddenly commonplace, unethereal, unspiritual, remotely unAthenian." She is old and she wants the Athenian to see this, but with the departure of her son she also feels curiously free. The son's acceptance of his poetic identity, his departure from the island and from his mother, lifts from her a clouded spirit; as a mother she finds freedom in the completion and union of the child's poetic gesture away from her. Her mirage and her reality, her doubled self, are also now allowed to meet in the completion of his poetic identity.

This novel richly defines a set of circumstances in H.D.'s own poetic development, particularly the sense of the doubled identity, the synonymous quality of mother and poetry, and the necessary presence of a male figure to validate the poetic gesture. Each of these elements surfaced in H.D.'s analysis with Freud, and were finally resolved in her favour as she consciously claims her poetic power.

In *Tribute to Freud*, H.D. says that she came to Freud to heal a sensed break in consciousness. To heal this doubleness and to let out what was beating in her brain, she navigated, with Freud's help, through the bell-jar experience, the writing-on-the-wall, her poetry, and her relation to her mother and father. As with Hedylus, this journey involved a shift in consciousness brought about by a man/god/father. For the first time in relation to a powerful male figure, H.D. recognizes the shape and intent of the power she longed to release in her work and she determines to own this power through the symbolic act of working through the mother energy embodied in a male figure. The power she longed for was not the power of sacred symbols she had acquired as a young child, prohibited from touching the tools of power on her father's desk, but the imaginative faculties acquired from her mother. "I want," she writes, "a fusion or a transfusion of my mother's art," a movement from the pre-verbal to the verbal.

H.D.'s analysis with Freud reads as a struggle between the two powers in her mind. Her choice of engaging in analysis is itself a struggle, as she reflects on Freud's belief that women by themselves do not amount to much creatively. From the beginning, she intuits an "argument implicit in our bones."

In *The Interpretation of Dreams*, Freud writes that he had "dared against the objections of severe science, to take the part of the ancients and of superstition." Elsewhere, he speaks of his discoveries paralleling the discovery of the Minoan and Mycenean civilizations that preceded the Greeks. Freud's science, like H.D.'s writing, was forged on women and on the realm of the feminine. Though they begin from the same source, the outcome of their enterprises diverge drastically. Freud intends to fix these superstitions in hard science, whereas H.D., as an artist and poet, devotes herself to following the images through to their own sense. Despite their differing intentions, H.D. finds in Freud someone who believes implicitly in the power of the realm she had previously tapped into with the bell-jar experience and the writing-on-the-wall. And on another, more important level, working with Freud allows her to wrest the power of the mother from a male figure where it resided in society at large and to claim this power and its symbols for herself.

This struggle culminates in the poem entitled "The Master," in which H.D. unveils a complete female artistic identity embodied in the image of the dancer:

I could not accept from wisdom
what love taught,
woman is perfect.
She is a woman,
yet beyond woman,
yet in woman,
her feet are the delicate pulse of the narcissus bud,
pushing from earth
(ah, where is your man-strength?)
her arms are the waving of the young
male,
tentative,
reaching out
that first evening
alone in a forest;
she is woman,
her thighs are frail yet strong,
she leaps from rock to rock
(it was only a small circle for her dance)
and the hills dance...

The line "woman is perfect" appears in another context, in *Tribute to Freud*, when Freud shows H.D. a small statue of Pallas Athene, whose winged embodiment is Nike or Victory.

One hand was extended as if holding a staff or rod. "She is perfect," he said, "only she has lost her spear."

Freud's gesture and comment bring up a string of associations: Pallas Athene, born of her father Zeus, making the judgement against her mother; goddess of war, now disarmed; perfect except for the lost spear, the mutilated female. H.D. takes these associations and transforms the figure in "The Master" poem to a complete figure of woman. The loss of the spear is the symbolic loss of the war mentality that had troubled H.D., and that appears as the baldest manifestation of patriarchal power's threatening global posture. Athene, goddess of war, is transformed into the dancer, whose knowledge and strength lies in the body's power of creativity; the energy of destruction is transformed to recall the energy of creation.

"The Master" closes with the line, "you are that Lord become woman," indicating that the transformation is complete as the dancer becomes the image of god. Thus, the Lord is no longer man and spirit, the Lord is woman, body, and nature. "That Lord become woman" will be accepted by everyone, men and women alike, and in that acceptance, men will realize how "this thought of the man-pulse has tricked them/has weakened them." In light of this, the woman/dancer/lord is life itself weakened by man/warrior/lord. H.D.'s placement of universal powers in women and in the body is a statement of what the world and men must know and recognize in order to survive. Her analysis leads her to the acceptance of her personal body and to a vision of life fragmented by the absence of women's holiness envisioned in the body. Through the confrontation of her own inability to accept the self as defined by her body, she comes to understand how this difficulty, which she perceived as personal, enters and affects the world at large. By recalling the life of the body, through the maternal, she is able to heal herself and to participate in healing the world.

PICTURE
ESSAY

Venus of Laussel, France, 25,000 – 20,000 B.C.E.
(Courtesy J.M. Arnaud, Musée d'Aquitaine, Bordeaux, France)

(Above) Women dancing, rock painting, Cogul, Spain, 10,000 B.C.E. (Courtesy The Metropolitan Museum of Art, Rogers Fund, 1912)

Prehistoric records of women dancing evoke the powers of the female body. Birth, death, and the relation to the vegetative and animal worlds are all expressed in these early images of women's dance activities.

(Right) Cycladic figure, C. 3,500 – 2,500 B.C.E. (Courtesy The Metropolitan Museum of Art, Gift of Christos G. Bastis, 1968)

(Left) *The Star* (Courtesy des Musées Nationaux, Paris)

(Below) *The Rehearsal of the Ballet*, Edgar Degas, 1875 (Courtesy The Nelson-Atkins Museum of Art, Kansas City, Missouri (Purchase: the Kenneth A. and Helen F. Spencer Foundation Acquisition Fund) F73-30)

Scene from George Balanchine's ballet, *Apollo* (Courtesy Martha Swope)

Scene from *The Red Detachment of Women*, China (Courtesy Performing Arts Research Center, New York Public Library at Lincoln Center)

Classical ballets cast women in roles that fail to acknowledge women's strength. As a sylph, a fairy, or a princess, the ballerina enacts narratives that undermine the actual power of her body. In revolutionary China, traditional ballet was transformed into a representation of female strength. Ballets featured heroines who struggled against brutality while the form showed women whose feet had been bound that great leaps were possible for all women.

(Left) Shinto temple dancer;
(Below) Shaker women dancing

(Courtesy Performing Arts
Research Center, New York
Public Library at Lincoln
Center.)

The expression of spirituality in dance is often entrusted to female worshippers.
In 17th century Japan, Shinto temple dancers introduced their dances into the
community in the form now known as Kabuki. In America, the Shakers, an
egalitarian Christian sect, featured dancing as part of their regular worship.

(Top) African initiation ritual; (Bottom) American initiation ritual
(Courtesy Lia Woods)

Initiation rites that mark the passage from girl to woman often involve
dancing. The dancing affirms the initiate's strength and her affinity to the
earth's power of fertility. In the puberty rite from the United States, young
girls perform a butterfly dance to symbolize their passage into womanhood.
The butterfly is an ancient goddess symbol that evokes the powers of
transformation.

(Right) German dancer and
choreographer Mary Wigman in
Witch Dance, 1914

(Below) American dancer and
choreographer Ruth St. Denis
in *Incense*, 1916

(Courtesy Performing Arts
Research Center, New York
Public Library at Lincoln Center)

The history of women in dance influenced the pioneers of modern dance in Europe and America. Ruth St. Denis made several trips to the Orient and integrated into her own work the spiritual qualities she recognized in ancient temple dances by women. Isadora Duncan was inspired by the ecstatic dances of the Greek Maenads whose rites had been outlawed during the emergence of the patriarchal state.

(Left) Roman copy of Greek Maenad (Courtesy The Metropolitan Museum of Art, Rogers Fund, 1923)

(Above) American dancer and choreographer Isadora Duncan, 1914 (Courtesy the Archives of the Isadora Duncan Foundation for Contemporary Dance, Inc.)

Modern dancers, Banff, Canada (Courtesy Banff School of Fine Arts)

The present work of women in dance explores the manisfestations of power in the female body and affirms the value of ritualizing experience through movement. Performers and non-performers alike engage in dance to create female-defined visions that re-member our bodies as centres of power and intelligence.

(Left) Sun Ock Lee
(Courtesy David
Fullard)

(Below) Sara Pearson
(Courtesy Nancy
Mellgren)

(Left) Maureen Fleming
(Courtesy Phil Trager)

(Below) Susana Galilea,
Three on a Donkey
(Courtesy Johan Elbers)

Pat Hall Smith, *Silent Echoes* (Courtesy Patented Photos)

(Above) Johanna Boyce and the Calfwomen, *Surrender, Mouth to Breast* (Courtesy Tom Brazil); (Below) Liz Lerman Dance Exchange, *This Is Who We Are* (Courtesy Beatriz Schiller)

VOICES
OF
THE
BODY

The idea for collecting these interviews arose from my desire to hear what other dancers had to say on the subject of women and dance. I asked the dancers I interviewed to tell me their stories. When did they start to dance? Did they like their bodies? How did they age with their bodies? Did their tradition give them room to explore their bodies as women? Was the "woman question" relevant to them? What had they learned from their daily work with the body? What did they want other women to know about their bodies? What was the history of their tradition? And what, if anything, did their tradition have to say about women?

Each of the dancers answered these questions as clearly and honestly as she could and I was struck by the single-minded devotion and love each dancer expressed for her chosen profession. Despite the fact of being poorly paid, (many dancers regularly rely on unemployment insurance as income— sometimes referring to it as a grant), of having to manage their careers on their own, of often having little energy left over for the creative work itself, each dancer expressed in passionate terms her love of dance and her attachment to the possibilities represented by the body.

I selected the dancers for the interviews based on my research and observation of different dance forms. I attended performances and took classes with some of the people I interviewed, partly to get another perspective on their work. Overall, I was struck by the dedication and devotion I heard expressed during the interviews, and with the energy of the performances and teachings. From the beginning, I knew I wanted to interview a Middle Eastern dancer. I had first seen Middle Eastern dance during a night-club show. Even in that setting, I immediately felt that this form kept alive the sensuality rooted in the wider creative experience of the female body. It was only much later that I discovered its history as a birth ritual. To my mind, classical Indian dance had the longest continuous story of women in dance. Also, I was intrigued by the luscious statues of classical Indian dancers and the complete belief by contemporary Indian dancers that they are reincarnations of these temple priestesses. African-American and African-Caribbean dance brought a strong sense of the spiritual, of that other world which dance can so easily move us into if we allow ourselves to be so moved. My interest in Butoh was piqued by a performance I attended with a friend. I had always thought of Butoh as a very bleak, male-centred dance form, yet Maureen Fleming clearly found much in it that enabled her to express a strong identification with nature. Though ballet and modern dance provided a more problematic representation of women and dance I felt they had to be included because they define dance for so many people. Each of these dance forms carried a part of the maternal/goddess heritage I had come to see during my research and I wanted to hear the living voice of this heritage.

Most of these dancers did not come by dance easily. Many of the non-Western dancers had families who were bitterly opposed to their dancing, often because dance was seen as a close cousin to prostitution. Sun Ock Lee's mother initially refused to send her daughter to dance class because only *kisaeng* or prostitutes danced. Ritha Devi's family opposed her ambition to be a dancer for the same reason. Until she finished college and was able to pay for her own lessons, Ritha danced in the privacy of her own room, frustrated by her lack of knowledge. "I had to fight against everybody else to dance," she told me. Anahid Sofian's mother, who eventually became an avid supporter, once called her daughter to ask if she was doing that "dirty Turkish dancing." Many of these women had mothers who realized how important dance was to their daughters and eventually managed to help them get to the resources they needed. The caricature of the ambitious ballet mother who pushes her daughter on stage to satisfy her own ambition does not appear in these stories. Here, mothers looked for teachers, studios, and theatres to help their daughters realize their yearning for dance.

For Western dancers, the difficulties came from another source. Without exception they had internalized the slender woman of Western culture. Always too fat, the body itself was the enemy. For the first time in an interview, Sara Pearson talks about her tortured relationship with food. We had agreed that she would talk freely during the interview and that I would give her the edited version for approval before publication. Her story is important for the very reason that it had been kept so secret. Susana Galilea and Johanna Boyce were direct in discussing this stereotype and its effect on their careers. Both of these dancers have had to reconcile their exceptional beauty as dancers with the unexceptional image of thinness still expected by many dance companies.

If these voices are so important, why have they not been heard? Dancers' lives reflect the value of the body and the value of women in this culture. It is women's work and it is neither well-paid, nor well-respected. But why have the women's movement and feminist theorists also not heard these voices? I still do not have an answer for this except to think that it is a measure of how deeply we have been turned against our bodies and how afraid we are of going to the knowledge of our bodies.

As dancers, these women are the voice of the body. And they are a voice which links us to our history and the knowledge of our bodies in the most living way I can think of.

PAT
HALL
SMITH

I first saw Pat Hall Smith in a solo piece she choreographed entitled Silent
Echoes. *At the time, I did not know that this piece was closely
autobiographical, the story of a dancer with a full-time job in the corporate
world. Video images of the dancer in a tailored business suit seated in a
conference room are set against the woman we see dancing on stage. Here,
she is an open and powerful woman in loose, comfortable clothes who owns
the space she is in. The juxtaposition brings out a contrasting set of values
and the ways in which these values are inscribed on the human body through
space and movement.*

*In 1987, Pat left her own corporate job to work full-time as a dancer.
Her training includes ballet, jazz, and African-Caribbean dance, which she
claims has had the strongest influence on her development. Her dedication
and persistence through strong opposition was repeated in the stories of dancers
I later interviewed. Pat admitted that it was very difficult for her to speak
about dance. "Dance is like breathing," she said. "How do you describe that
and what it is to you? It's like life itself." In the following narrative, Pat
tells how she made the transition from the corporate to the dance world and
how she has worked to integrate aspects of her life as a dancer, choreographer,
and mother.*

In my work I'm trying to take a universal approach, to tell a story
through dance. I'm not interested in just being "visible" as a dancer. I
feel that I have to speak about what's happening in life and how it has
affected me.

I was raised in New York and I started to study dance when I was nine. At that time most schools offered either ballet or modern dance. I wasn't exposed to jazz or "ethnic" dance until I was a teenager. Charles Moore was the first teacher who introduced me to West African and Caribbean dance. It was the first time that my body felt comfortable with a dance style.

In ballet and modern I always felt out of place. I felt restricted, constricted. I would always want to move to the music a little bit more than the teacher thought was appropriate. I wanted the freedom to interpret the music more fully. It wasn't until I got involved in "ethnic dance," dance with drums, that I really started to feel something happening in my body.

Very early on I felt that I had something to share with people. I wanted the exchange with an audience. I think of the performance as a piece that has to reach people. It has to first start inside. The motivation of the dance has to reach someplace inside of me before I can communicate with the audience. A reviewer in *Dance Magazine* once said that I opened myself to the audience, I took a chance. That's what I try to do. When I take such a risk, I often can sense an emotional response and a kind of unspoken understanding from the audience. It's not just my own experience that I'm bringing to the performance.

Each time you decide to take the performance plunge, you risk everything. There was a time when I was more concerned about what people wanted to see. I didn't know what that was. Now it's more important to me to try to be honest with myself. Even in my classes I try to do that. I try to encourage an exchange of energy and spirit between the students and myself in response to the drummers. I like my body. When I'm dancing I'm exploring my sexuality, sensuality, my power. Dancing has helped me to grow as a person. It's the one time I feel whole and complete, not afraid of anything. I enjoy feeling my centre. It's my temple, where I worship and where I'm safe. I enjoy the feelings that brings me. The ritual aspect of the Haitian dances has affected me deeply, with its combination of sacred symbolism and sensuality. The Haitian dances use every part of the body in both subtle and expansive movements. I hear the relationship between the beat of my heart and the beat of the drum.

There have been times when I haven't felt safe in dance. It's a challenge, like living day to day. It changes, although I'm enjoying it more these days than I have in the past. For me, dance is life and living, and when things are not right in the outside world, dance is my inside world. It affects how I move, how I feel, how I view myself and how I think other people view me. It's uncomfortable when I don't really feel connected to my emotions and to my movement.

Having my daughter changed my sense of my body. I felt it as I was pregnant. I became more aware of my pelvis, more in touch with it, and enjoyed what I was feeling. I felt like a woman. I really became aware of that area as being the centre, the life-force. I can see it in women who are pregnant or who have children. They actually move from there. It's like a flower blossoming. It starts to grow, and it just opens up. It grows through the entire body. Everything is alive.

When I choreograph for myself, I start with a theme and try to develop movement based on that theme or idea. The theme may express something about a social issue, or who we are. I go with whatever is happening in the moment. Choreographing requires accepting the power you have and the power you may have over other people. It's difficult to do that, because I'm vulnerable. I'm presenting myself. This is what I have to say, this is the statement that I am making.

I quit my corporate job in 1987. During my last few years there, I started to teach, and the demands of the job started to interfere with my teaching commitments. I had to make a decision. On my first trip abroad, I decided I couldn't go back, that dance really meant everything to me and I was dying in my job. I've never regretted the decision. The only time I felt alive was when I would dance. Since making that decision, I have received growing support from family, friends, and sponsors. In particular, Dance Theatre Workshop provided a grant for research and performance opportunities.

I have to be accepting of the changes in my body as I get older. I

123

have injured my knees. The healing process is slow. I'm trying to just live, to accept life each day, to accept this body. Movement takes on a whole other shape, and sometimes that's good. I'm living with my body. I'm growing into my body.

ANAHID
SOFIAN

In the early nineties, a lawyer in Egypt petitioned the Egyptian government to outlaw belly dancing. Since the Egyptian constitution is built on Islamic law which states that a woman is allowed to show her body only to her husband, this lawyer argued that belly dancing violated the constitution. This action is the latest in a series of attempts throughout history to regulate or outlaw belly dancing. Originally, belly dancing was a birth ritual, and it presents a model of women completely in charge of the creative powers of their bodies. This aspect of the dance shines through even in the most inhospitable settings, and it explains why the dance has attracted so much opposition.

Anahid Sofian, a performer, choreographer, and teacher of Middle Eastern dance for nearly thirty years, remarked that the dance always evokes a strong audience reaction, whether positive or negative. Of Armenian descent, Anahid had never seen belly dancing until her twenties when she was introduced to it by a cousin. She immediately fell in love with it and embraced it as her life work.

I studied with Anahid for several years, and she is a gifted and caring teacher. She attributes her devotion to teaching to the fact that she had to learn the dance on her own when she started. All kinds of women come through her studio, living proof that this oldest dance link to our maternal heritage still has much to offer women of all ages and types.

The Middle Eastern dancers have such an enjoyment of their body and of being female. They project a femininity and a sexuality that is not a come-on kind of thing. It's what we call an Oriental head. It's also the way they interpret the music. American dancers work very hard at technique and they're better dancers in terms of the range of technique.

They take it very seriously as an art form but often they leave out this very personal, subjective aspect of it.

In my experience, women study Middle Eastern dance to get more in touch with their bodies. It's a great fun way of exercising and it makes them feel very good, too. It's exhilarating and it frees you. I've had women tell me that they've felt changes in their pelvises once they break through certain movements, especially the undulation which moves through the pelvis. It's freeing to move the pelvis in this way, and you may not even realize that you are restricted in your body. The dance has a fluidity and pelvic centring to it.

I started to dance as a child. My mother saw dance ability in me when I was young, but my father was very repressive. I'm Armenian and they were old world survivors of the Turkish genocide. My father was especially repressive. It was just the way he was— that respectable women didn't dance.

My mother wanted to give me dance classes when I was very young because she saw that I loved to move. As a child, I remember responding to music. It was so natural. That was enough for my mother, but my father did not take my dancing seriously and I started to develop some health problems. I wet my bed, I developed a nervous tick all along the side of my face and the back of my neck. No matter how much I ate I was underweight. (I remember my mother feeding me butter.) The doctor said, "It's nerves. Give her dance classes for health reasons. Get her to exercise and move her body." I was a very obstinate child and my father finally started me in ballet. If I was going to do a dance form, it was going to be the most aesthetic, demanding. I truly did love it and I progressed very rapidly: I stopped wetting my bed, the tick started to go away. They put me on pointe very fast and I started to learn *Swan Lake*. I was taking tap, acrobatics, and ballet at the local school.

In my teens I discovered boys and my dancing fell by the wayside. I also came into contact with modern dance at my high school. I was invited to have a scholarship when I was fifteen years old but I didn't pursue it. I got side-tracked with boys and I got married as soon as I was eighteen. Part of the problem and part of the reason was to get away from my father. It was not the right escape but I really was in love and I was seventeen, so what else could I do? I was married for six or seven years before we separated. I got married quickly a second time but at that time I also started to study dance again. I always danced at home. It was always part of my life. I'd put music on and would still continue dancing, but I hadn't taken classes for all those years. My second husband was a musician and encouraged me to go back and I did go back full-time.

I went back to ballet and also began studying modern dance. My teacher encouraged me to go professional. I was working very intensely, taking seven classes a week, sometimes twice a day. Then I joined a modern dance company. My modern was very weak since my major training was ballet; modern is a very different technique with different placement. I was working at a professional level but I really didn't have the control, the technique, or the strength yet. And I developed knee trouble, which became chronic. I didn't give it any thought. I had taken my body very much for granted and I continued dancing and taking classes. When I moved back to New York I was practically crippled and I finally went to a doctor. My thigh muscles had atrophied and I had no circulation in my legs. I hobbled into the doctor's office and he wanted to do cortisone treatments. I said no. I was in my mid-twenties and I had to give up dancing for three years because I would not do the cortisone treatment. We started with ultra-sound, then exercising with weights tied to my feet. It was gruelling. That's how I went into belly dancing, as a form of physical therapy.

As a child I had never seen belly dancing and I wasn't interested. I was madly in love with classical dance and that's what I was after. And I had an attitude. Ballet dancers can be terrible snobs. I really thought ethnic dance was at a lower level. I had never seen a belly dancer. It was not in our culture. I grew up hearing Middle Eastern music at home, but certainly the attitude toward belly dance was that it was a dirty Turkish thing. In New York, as my legs were healing, the doctor said I should do some kind of dance but not ballet. I started to go folk-dancing and I was going to some Middle Eastern clubs with my cousin. When I saw my first belly dancer it totally blew me away. Her name was Athena. I thought it was one of the most beautiful, most powerful dance forms I had ever seen. I became obsessed with it and I started to teach myself. I was going every night, but I was afraid to approach anybody. The dancers all looked forbidding. In those years, in the sixties, there were a lot of clubs. It was a very rich period in New York. I was obsessed with it and started going practically every night.

I would come home and try out the movements in front of a mirror. I practised endlessly and then I developed tendonitis in my hips because I was overdoing it. So I had to stop again for a few months. I remember how hard it was breaking through my ballet training in my torso. Finally after about a year I took some private lessons with an American dancer with whom I established a friendship. She told me to get a job, which I did. I decided to go professional and take it seriously. I never did get back to ballet, but I started to study at the Erick Hawkins studio because I felt his dance technique was compatible with the Oriental.

The clubs were Greek, Arab, or Persian owned and you walked into another culture. I had to subdue my personality to work in these clubs. In the day-time I was working at *Saturday Review* magazine as an editorial assistant and that job kept my sanity because the attitude toward the dancers was terrible. You really were the lowest of the low. The musicians and club owners were very ambivalent. On the one hand, they love the dance, but they have a very low opinion of the dancers. You had to fight really hard to get respect.

This dance exists on so many different levels. I've always found what it brings out in people to be very revealing. To me it's a completely natural, organic, feminine dance; men do it too, but it developed primarily as a female dance. And I think it can be very threatening— to both men and women. I've had people be hostile to me in audiences. I'm not vulgar and I'm not out to titillate. It can be used as titillation but that's not what its intent is. And it exists from the street level to whore-houses to the concert stage. The level depends entirely on the artist, on the dancer. To me it has evolved into a truly beautiful art form that has its cultural aspects. As hard as people like myself and others in the field have tried, it still has a lousy reputation.

In a way it was very hard to break in. There weren't that many dancers and it was a very closed society among the dancers. There were no schools in those days. Either you learned by yourself or if you were lucky to make friends with a dancer she would take you in as a protégé. That's how this dance form has been handed down over the years. It was their way of keeping phonies out; you had to prove yourself to everybody. And if the audience liked you they threw money which went to the musicians and to the house. The musicians were given the money because they were paid a small salary. The dancer was paid fairly decently, better than they are paid today. If you drew good tips, the musicians played well for you.

The dance had a low life image attached to it and that's why I wanted to take it out of the night-clubs, to go for another level. There is an excitement to dancing in a cabaret setting that you don't get on a concert stage because there is a real interaction with the audience. But I felt it had to make another statement and I did two performances in the sculpture garden of the Museum of Modern Art. Then I opened my studio. I had an opportunity to jump ship with my day-time job so I opened my studio and started to face financial disaster.

Belly dancing has such an incredible range of material. You can interpret it and put it together so many ways with many different costumes. Don McDonagh, a reviewer at the New York Times, called it a suite of dances, and he's absolutely right. There are five or more different musical changes. The dancer has to learn these rhythms and they all convey a different mood and utilize a specific vocabulary. The dance can express sadness, it can be exuberant. It has a range of feelings, depending on the dancer's interpretive range. It's quite complete and satisfying. People think it's one step above stripping, that it almost belongs to burlesque, but it really doesn't have that effect. Burlesque is meant to titillate and get men turned on. This dance doesn't do that. It turns you on but it also comes around and has a finish. A stripper takes her clothes off and that's the end of it, but belly dancing builds up to the point. The middle is very sensual and beautiful but then it becomes lively again at the end. It's a very complete experience. One of the most beautiful things about it is that it is completely individualistic; you can interpret it. Six women can do the same movement and it will look totally different, acceptable, and wonderful.

Floor work is my favourite part of the dance. It's emotionally very powerful. It also requires a lot of physical power. It is almost banned now because people see it as crawling around on the floor, Hollywood style, grovelling. I don't see it that way, but I do agree that if it isn't done well, it can look vulgar. I just know how emotionally I experienced it as powerful. In the Middle East, women gave birth on their knees. I feel that had something to do with that section of the dance evolving, getting down to the floor. It's also natural for such an earthy dance to have a floor section.

The dance is definitely tied up with childbirth, there's no question about it. It's been done for thousands of years primarily for women by women. I think the floor section is an outgrowth of that. I also associate it with a snake on the floor. Emotionally it's very powerful and deep. It's like you're deeply into the dance and into yourself. I think it's very threatening because you are at your most powerful. I stretch my body to the maximum during that section so my energy is very focused. Nobody is allowed to do floor work in the Middle East. They want to be entertained by this dance and it should stay within certain boundaries, keep emotions within certain boundaries. It has a very mesmerizing effect. Physically, it's very hard to do, so I don't even teach it much in class because a lot of the students can't do it, but I wish I had somebody I could really work with to pass that on to, someone who could bring that back.

In Egypt, dancers have to cover the mid-section of the body. Dancers got around that by wearing netting or sheer silk which in a way is even more provocative. The costume is also an artistic expression and is perfectly suited to the dance— the scarves on the hips to show the hip work, the beadwork down the front to show the undulation. That was one of the things I fell in love with. A costume is a work of art.

Great care is taken with costumes. It's not like modern dance where you just put on a leotard. The costume is very integrated with the dance. Cabaret dancers are most maligned because they are uncovered and do provocative movements out in the open to a mixed audience. There are dancers in Egypt called *Awalem* and these women would never dream of putting on a belly dancing costume and going into a night-club. They're completely covered. The costume changes the dance totally. They're hired for weddings and parties and often they will hire one dancer for the men and one for the women. *Awalem* means "those who instruct," so they are hired for weddings to give the bride some instruction too as part of their job, and they're very respected.

I kept my dancing secret and my parents didn't know I was a belly dancer. I just never told them. I danced for years and my father passed away and then my mother heard about it. There was an article about me in an Armenian newspaper and she called me up and asked, "Are you doing that dirty Turkish dancing?" My mother is extremely open-minded but that's how she said it. And I said, "No, Ma, I'm doing classical Arabic style dancing," and that was okay. Now she's a great fan. She adores the dance and she loves Turkish music. She's very musical herself and sings Turkish music, but there was something in her that reacted. She got past it, though. I think my father would have disowned me.

There definitely was companionship and friendship among the dancers once you were accepted. They sewed costumes for each other. Turkish dancers did beadwork like nobody I've ever seen. Egyptians have their style of costume making but they don't work with bugle beads that much. Turkish dancers made netting with bugle beads. They made jackets, harem pants. It was absolutely stunning, and now it's a lost art because nobody knows how to do it any more.

My field is very fragmented right now. The Arabs stay together, the Turks stay together, the Greeks stay together, the Armenians stay together. They are in their own little communities and they play their own music. In the sixties, it was incredibly rich because everybody learned everybody else's music. The Arabs played Turkish music, the Greeks played Arab music, the Turks played Greek music, and the Armenians played all of it. The bands were mixed, the dance styles were mixed. I still mourn those days. It's so clear in my head: the sharing, mutual appreciation, and love. Now there is no such thing as a Middle Eastern club in this city. You go to an Egyptian club and that's all they play. They don't even play other Arabic music. They only play Egyptian music. I certainly feel like it's very fragmented with everyone fighting so hard for their own identities.

I love what I do. I am a dancer. This is my medium and I just love it. I don't think I could have grown if I had stayed in classical ballet. It was one of those life-changing things that happened by accident because of an injury. I had to stop ballet and I never did go back. There is no end to this dance. I get bored with certain aspects but I look for other avenues of expression and it keeps growing the deeper I get into it.

I have always liked my own body. I had a great deal of vanity in my youth. I had a very nice body. I was told that a lot and I liked that. It's interesting, though, because as free as I thought I was, I detested veil work when I first started to dance and perform. I still remember that moment of panic when I had to take the veil off. In those days, with the cabaret routine, you came out covered and then took the veil off. I felt so vulnerable. I thought I was so free in my body, but I wasn't. At that moment I wanted to hide, because it's a moment when you're starting to reveal yourself. But I got past it and I love veil work now.

As a professional and an artist I'm sad at what's gone as I've gotten older. My timing is slower. I don't have the agility, I don't have the speed, but one thing that's really great about this dance form is the older you get the better you are. There's a maturity that has to come with it and the most popular dancers in the Middle East are not the young beautiful dancers with the great bodies. The most popular are the older dancers, because their interpretation, maturity, and emotional development come through. This dance is very revealing about who you are and what you are. It's not like ballet, with a high-powered technique you can hide behind. It's very total. There's a confidence and a poise that you just don't have in your youth. In that respect I feel I have gotten to be a better dancer as I've gotten older, but I've lost a lot of what I can control. I still feel I'm capable of a great deal and I think it's because of the nature of this dance. It's so natural and organic for the body.

I get a lot back from teaching. I do like to teach very much. Sometimes I wish I didn't have to teach so much and I feel very unbalanced. I wish I could perform more and create more artistically. I create for the classroom but it's not the same. But there's enough gratification and it really is beautiful to watch people walk in here hardly able to tell their right foot from their left. Breakthroughs happen in class. So I get a lot back and we have a very wide range of ages and body types. You can come to it at any point in your life, at any age, and get something out of it. That's another beautiful thing about it. People work at their own level with it. I can't think of another dance form that can really give you that. It's accessible. That doesn't mean it's simple. It's very accessible and all women can relate to it. Essentially, it's a woman's dance.

SUN
OCK
LEE

I first saw Sun Ock Lee perform a dance meditation at an international dance festival hosted by La Mama Theatre in New York. Although the performance took place almost ten years ago, I remember vividly a very delicate and surprising dropping motion woven into a slow meditative dance. I was surprised by the tiny woman who greeted me at The Asia Society where she has been artist-in-residence for twenty years. On stage she appeared larger than life. Of all the dancers I interviewed, Sun Ock Lee is the only one who insisted that I get up and move to experience a point she was trying to make. She urged me to stand up and vigorously shake my hands and feet as she spoke of the importance of movement for women and its ability to redirect the flow of energy in our bodies. Her own choreography is a synthesis between her traditional and contemporary background. In a piece called Lotus, she dances bare-breasted to make a statement about the binding of women's breasts in the traditional Korean dance costume.

When I was nine, I went to a dance studio for the practice of Korean dance, and I was totally lost. I couldn't think of anything else so I told my mother that I wanted to learn. My mother said no, that dance was only for *kisaeng*. *Kisaeng* is the counterpart of geishas in Japan. In those days, if you were from a long-born or aristocratic family you were not supposed to dance. Commoners or the servant class could dance, so my family would not allow me to dance, but I was so taken I just couldn't think of anything else.

From the age of nine I knew I would be a dancer and I knew I would come to America. I just pursued it and finally my mother said okay. She was a very wise woman. She was a strong Buddhist and she practised meditation. She was a bit intuitive and knew my life would be the life of an artist so she encouraged me to dance. We didn't have money because we moved from North Korea to South Korea during the war. My father died and my mother had seven children to care for. Everyone had to go to school and if you were good you got a scholarship; otherwise, you could not go. All my brothers and sisters were able to get scholarships. That's how it began. War made us into survivors.

In Korea, traditional dance is taught very much from a guru to a student. My teacher is now a national living treasure. I studied with Master Mei-Bang Lee, and with the late Paek-Cho Kim, the first Korean woman to study Martha Graham's technique in America. Korean dance is very different from Western dance. Ballet and modern dance are very demonstrative, outgoing, and experimental. In a way, they are very much designed for audiences, whereas Korean dance is very spiritual and internal. It is Taoist and Zen-like. One must be totally committed to become one with her own self. In other words, you have to be in a state of total awareness and total transformation, almost a state of emptiness. Then, because you become so pure, whatever you are reflecting will reflect on the audience.

The aesthetic is totally different. The manner in Korean dance is introverted, and whatever you do is an ultimate exclamation, even flicking the sleeve or turning the hands is like a period at the end of a sentence, rather than a continuous dynamic of movement. It prolongs movement and then makes a certain curve or an exclamation with gestures or the feet. Korean dance is very subtle in a very delicate way. It is not very gestural, like Japanese or Indian dance. It is much more abstract and symbolic. It's total integration with the breath and letting the breath express itself through your whole body.

When teachers train you they don't tell you what to do. You just do it. The teacher will dance in front of you and you must follow. Repeat, repeat, and repeat. Now and then she will correct you, but in those days teachers didn't explain because they were not very intellectual.

The dances were just learned and teachers didn't analyze. They didn't try to find out why you didn't do it or why you did it well. I was just lucky I was able to perceive movement and I just did it. I added my own style, which is permitted in Korean dance. In Korean dance, once you master the elementary level and all the basic movement, you have to come up with your own style, otherwise you are not considered a good ʼɔncer. They allow your personality, your characteristics to enter in the ʲation. Of course you have to stay within that context but it gives you tremendous freedom conceptually.

There are very, very few male dancers in Korea even today. Korea was predominantly a male society and men who danced were considered to be sissies. It was not even considered, but there are always exceptions. My teacher, Mae-Bang Lee, was male. Male dancers tend to be very feminine, but there are distinctive male dances like mask dances or certain court dances. Historically, there were roles for male dancers. Some of the folk dances, mask dance dramas, and farmers' dances were all performed by males. When it comes to folklore, there are more male dancers. Their movements are more active and bigger, contrary to the female movements. There aren't many men and women pair movements. That came later, during the nineteenth century, with the influence of the West.

Basically, Korean dance comes from either Buddhist ritual, performing arts, or from shamanistic rituals. There are twelve different ceremonies in one shamanistic ritual and there are many different types of shamanistic rituals based on the different regional styles. Those shamanistic ritual performances, court dances, and Buddhist rituals combined to make up Korean dance.

Korean shamans are like psychiatrists in this society. In those days, the science of medicine was not developed. If a child was dying, people would automatically go to the shaman and the shaman would pray to the gods— the mountain god, the dragon god, or the heavenly god. They would just pray and sometimes it worked and sometimes it didn't. There were male shamans but the majority of them were female. I think shamans were very much entertainers as well as social healers. They could play the role of psychologist, doctor, and entertainer.

The movements depend on the shamanistic ritual. For instance, there are two types of shamanistic rituals in Korea. In one ritual the shaman is a mediator between the dead and living spirits. In that case, the movements are very violent: jumping, hopping, and twisting. In the southern part of Korea the shamans are trained to sing, chant, and dance. They are more like dancers.

When I was nine or ten I loved everything about dance. I loved my ballet toe shoes. I remember when I had my first toe shoes. They were made out of wood and all my skin peeled from dancing on wooden shoes. We used meat to protect our feet. We wrapped nylon stockings around the meat and put it inside the toe shoe. I remember one rainy day I couldn't wear shoes because my skin was all peeled off and my feet were bleeding so I had to walk on bare feet.

I couldn't think of anything else but dance. When I look at somebody's face I think of putting make-up on. I look at fabric and I think of costumes. If I look at light I think of stage lighting. I was like that. Dance was everything to me, and I started to choreograph at the age of eleven. In elementary school I choreographed mask games. I created festivals, and when I entered junior high I formed a dance group. I taught every day after school. When I was thirteen or fourteen I already had won an award in a national dance contest. My interest was only dance. I didn't have time for men. I wasn't interested in men. All of my friends wanted to go out with men, and said to me that they were so charming and handsome, but I couldn't understand why.

I loved modern dance— I think that's why I started to create Zen dance— except I knew that modern dance was started and built on Western body structures. For an Asian, the sensitivity to the music and rhythm might be good but structure-wise the body is weak compared to Westerners. If you look at American or European women they are very tall, whereas Asian women's bodies are thinner and more fragile, with shorter legs.

I came to America in 1969. There was a world exposition in Montreal and I brought my dance group. Then I decided to come to America to study so I applied to New York University to go to school. In 1978, New York University asked me to teach Korean dance. Meanwhile, I formed my own company and opened a studio theatre in 1976 in Manhattan. I was also doing traditional Korean dance at The Asia Society. I have been resident artist at The Asia Society for the past twenty years and I have been performing all over, in schools, theatres, museums, zoos, and libraries.

My own choreography is a synthesis between my contemporary background and my traditional background. In being exposed to all these Asian and European dances, I learned about myself, who I am, what I am, what I like to do. That is the main issue of all education: to understand ourselves and find our essence and relationship between society and our selves.

In Korea I had teachers, teachers, teachers! I couldn't get away. If you are a good student, a scholarship student or heir to a technique, you just cannot be on your own. That's why I came here, because I learned I would never get out from under that tradition. When I came here, I entered a Buddhist temple because my mother was Buddhist and it made me feel at home. Once I started meditating I went from sitting meditation to walking meditation to movement meditation to dance meditation. It was a very natural outcome.

Over the last twenty years I have developed a meditation technique which shows people how to transform the Ki. Ki is made up of the air you inhale and the food you eat. Food creates blood and blood is carried by the air you inhale. Those two components become the Ki. In English, a similar term is vapour or energy. This will be controlled by your thoughts. When you are angry, all your blood goes to your head and that's why a lot of people have strokes and heart attacks. If you can control the Ki, control the blood by sending it to your abdominal region rather than to your head, you can change how you feel and easily find an equilibrium of emotion. I developed a breathing technique to transform the Ki from your lower abdominal region to all parts of your body. You meditate on the process of your Ki flow. It's very much like meditation. Once dancers train in this way, they no longer dance by thinking of the sequence of movements, thinking how is my body going to be. They concentrate on the process of the Ki flow within the body. Then you don't have to worry about how you move; everything is in your collective memory, what I call memory consciousness. Movements are recorded in your memory and unwind like a tape recorder. Whatever is stored in your memory will manifest into a movement creation.

I go into a series of meditations, lying on the floor, first how to concentrate on lower abdominal region breathing and then how to transform the Ki to different parts of the body. There are a series of contraction and release exercises in the lower abdominal region to develop an awareness of sending energy to different parts of your body. It becomes self-healing and self-therapy in a way. The third part is how to create the movement from a thought and how to go back to the root of a thought. For example, if you are angry, you look for your anger. Where is it coming from? You cannot see it, you cannot touch it, and yet you are angry. What is the self reacting to? When you go back to that you have no answer. This is called Zen quest. In the next stage of technique, your feelings and thoughts are replaced by the root of each thought, and this is another stage of how you enter your thoughts, how you cut through your thinking process and incorporate this into movement. Whatever you are doing becomes the embodiment of the meditation. That is why I call it dance meditation. The whole idea is how to empty yourself, how to be in touch with your pure self, and then everything can be accepted and everything can be utilized without any resistance. The higher goal is to relate that theory in practical life. When you are angry and you don't like things you can control your emotions. So it becomes very practical, from actual dance movements and dance meditation to practical life.

Choreography is all process. For dancers who trained in ballet and modern dance it takes a long time. They want to kick their legs, they want to jump and turn, they want to show off whatever they learned. They have to let it all go to really dwell in their energy flow, then whatever you want to do becomes like an organic process. When you watch how the bean sprout grows, you don't see it growing every second. It's the same way in movement. You have to watch for the slow process of your organic process. A growing process, that's how I train them. It takes time and sometimes young dancers are very restless. You struggle and give up, then you really begin. Individuals have different barriers and I have to deal with each individual. Sometimes I have to conquer them, sometimes I have to talk to them. Many different techniques are required. Some dancers have nightmares or start to cry— their memories of sad experiences start to come out all of a sudden. Or some of them experience cramps in their stomachs because they are not used to using very deep lower muscles.

I didn't start meditation to become a guru or a Zen master. I only studied because I wanted to know who I am and to enrich my creativity. I think my function in this life is to be a dancer and choreographer, so I stay in that realm. Although I have a Zen temple where I live, and I meditate every morning and chant with my daughter, my emphasis is not to become a guru so I function in lay society.

Lotus is my Buddhist name from my Zen master, Song Dahm. Lotus symbolizes the pure flower with its root embedded in mud which symbolizes our desires— food, sex, material wealth. The desires are the ground and the mud; the lotus flower does not exist if you cut the stem. In the same way, your desire, your attachment is the source of practice. I believe these are the actual ingredients of my practice and what I am doing. My new piece is about taming the bull, which refers to a reflection of yourself and your thinking and illusions. Taming actually is just a name for conflicting with your own self.

In a way, choreography is a mediation, and the practice in itself evolves with a life, relationships, my friends, the artists I work with.

Anything can happen: my choreography is my life. It's just a matter of how and what aspects of my life I will put on stage. It all ties into the meditation and the practice of meditation.

I always compare my work habits to a pregnancy. When you are pregnant it takes time to mature once you conceive. It just goes on and when it has to come out it has to come out, no matter what. At some points, I feel I don't do anything, but somehow, something conceived in my mind just grows subconsciously. I believe in the subconscious life of human psychology. I don't worry about it. It grows and just happens.

When I'm performing I don't feel a separation at all between myself and the audience. American audiences go bananas when they watch these slow Zen dances. First, they think something is going to happen but nothing happens. It just keeps going. Finally they give up. Then they start to watch each movement organically and then they are mesmerized. Some people are mesmerized from the beginning as if hypnotized and some are not. This is something I think I am experiencing with the audience. The audience comes with the expectation to be entertained. I don't do that. I want them to meditate with the dancers, even though I try to incorporate all those dynamics in different realms of art, painting, sounds, and instruments. For example, where the movement is slow the instruments are loud so I make a juxtaposition of different dynamics. I do everything counter to my movements. My movements may be very simple and monotonous but I enter other elements to counterbalance. It is just like the rock and the waterfall. The rock doesn't do anything but the water falls and creates a dynamic. This is the phenomenon of the universe, where everything harmonizes and creates its own dynamics. This is something I'm consciously or subconsciously developing and aware of when I create.

I know if the audience is with me or not but I have to learn to screen it out. I just have to meditate, no matter what goes on. Some of the audience may fall asleep immediately because they are so tired or they cannot deal with it or they feel peaceful. They come and may fall asleep which is okay because their minds or bodies may need to rest.

Performing is like my life. I can't picture myself not doing it as long as my body permits. It's the best therapy. One of the beauties of this dance is the detachment or freeing from one's possessions or obsessions. It means overcoming your age and your limitations so old age doesn't mean a thing. No matter what you look like you present the best of yourself. That is when you are in touch with your own purity of self and it manifests itself. It all depends on how you transcend yourself to purity because that state of eternity— the purity— doesn't age. What exists before your thinking doesn't age— it's there— so when you go into that state or trance your age is not going to matter. Once the dancer understands that all dancers have shamanistic elements— the ability to channel and communicate between the universal energy and the human energy— then time disappears.

In Buddhism you do maternity education or fertility education. When my baby was conceived I chanted and meditated every day because I was giving my energy to the baby. I felt like we were responding to each other— even today my daughter and I are so close. I really feel that she understands me better than anybody. I feel that women are blessed in that way. Men will never have that experience. Men understand fatherhood or what a parent's love is like later, by watching children grow, but women, because they go through the sensation of birthing a child, are much closer with human contact and therefore embrace it. And yet, because of that pain, women can be more attached to things and become more neurotic and difficult. They have more collective experiences that hinder them from becoming pure and simple. Women are more complex. Even Buddha says there are two hundred and fifty regulations for monks and about five hundred for nuns. The complexity of our body structure creates more thinking ability and difficulty of detachment. Men are built in a more simple way and find it easier to deal with things.

Dance definitely has particular things to teach women. First of all breathing, contracting and releasing through the lower abdominal region gives terrific childbirth muscle training for women and it's also very sensuous. A woman can contract and pull in her vagina and do tremendous things like get rid of cold symptoms and discharges.

Spiritually as well. Stress, anger, sadness— it sets in our body. I can see the human body and I can see where people carry their tension. I became like a doctor. I see dancers and I see where they tend to build tension in their bodies. You have to learn to release and let the blood circulate properly. I see many people abuse their bodies. This whole culture is abusive. Modern society is suffering, whereas before, you could read Shakespeare, you could hear Tchaikovsky or Brahms and you could be satisfied. The ultimate goal of all good arts is to build a release system and it's therapeutic, but today people build themselves up without sufficient release. That is one of the reasons I am doing Zen dance, to reach the realm of serenity and equilibrium. After you shake it up and get all sweaty, then what? In order to rest we need exercises, not only jogging or vigorous exercises but exercises that calm and tune our bodies in peace and put us at ease. Simple methods can rejuvenate your whole system, so yes, I think women should practise Zen dance.

RITHA
DEVI

After our interview, Ritha Devi called me to add one more comment: "The indomitable female spirit has kept me going all these years," she said. "I do think of myself as a reincarnated temple dancer. I have that attitude. I feel myself consecrated to the temple." Like many classical Indian dancers I have seen, Ritha has a very sure and calm knowledge of the strength of the female spirit. Her work is about recovering this female spirit and giving it form through retelling the stories of the goddesses and heroines who populate Indian mythology.

Ritha received her training from a guru who is a direct descendant of the temple dancers, and she has recovered and performed a cycle of dance-dramas, Panchakanya, from the repertoire of the Devadasis. Her performances usually begin and end with an invocation to Durga, the Mother-Goddess, destroyer of sins, vanquisher of demons, and protector of all who seek refuge from her.

When I first called Ritha inquiring about an interview, she cautioned me that, "The body is important but the body is not the be all and end all. You've got to surpass the body and come into something higher."

Nobody pushed me to dance. In fact, I had to fight against everybody else to dance. I did not start as a child. I got the passion for it by seeing Uday Shankar. I found it absolutely fascinating and from then on I started this love affair with dance. It was a love affair because it was a total obsession with me. But I wasn't allowed to dance by my family. My parents didn't think that I, as a good family girl, should take to dance. In those days, they still looked down upon it, and also they insisted that I finish my education, so I had to wait all those years until I finished college. I just did what little I could in the privacy of my room. My parents would go out in the evening and I would secretly try and do something on my own. I knew nothing but what I would imagine and I made up little dances and this passion continued with me. It was very frustrating because I knew that I had it in me, and yet without the proper training I wasn't developing.

I didn't start any classical dance training until after I finished college which was fairly early. By that time, my father had retired and we went all the way across to the Northeast where they wanted to settle down after father's retirement. And there I came across this beautiful style called Manipuri. Manipuri is a special place on the borderline between India and Burma, and at last I was free to dance. So I got together with a few other people and I managed to bring a guru over to where we were living, but within a week my parents took their word back. Father said he didn't have that much money to squander. So I said, if you don't have money to pay for my dance training, then I will earn it, which was unthinkable in those days— a good family girl going to work. So I taught dance to little children and from that money I paid for my own dance training. From then till now I have not taken a cent from anybody towards my dance training, because that attitude continued. My parents wanted to get me married. They didn't want me to sit at home and dance so they got me married and that made things worse. I had made it very clear to my would-be husband that dance was a passion with me and I wanted to continue with it. He more or less lied, saying that he was going to help me and he didn't. The moment he got married to me, he changed his tune and put on a different appearance altogether, and I was quite shocked because I had trusted him. It was then I realized that I just had to fight my way in order to keep up dance.

When we got married, we came down to Calcutta where he was posted at that time and my guru just came by himself with his assistant in the hope I would look after him. I couldn't possibly turn him back. Whatever idea I may have had about keeping domestic peace by giving up dance dissipated when I saw my guru come to stand at the gate one night waiting for me. You're supposed to more or less look after your guru. It's expected that you will look after him, not just monetarily, but give him all his comforts. It doesn't finish with giving your fee for the class. The guru becomes a father image to the student.

Dance was the only way I could express myself. My body was crying out to dance and from my tentative early clumsy movements I gradually honed and polished and perfected my art entirely through my own discipline. No guru ever disciplined me the way I disciplined myself. I got to the stage where I could be proud of what I was doing. That has taken literally years.

It was a very difficult situation because I was newly married and I never got approval from my husband for my dance. When the neighbours sometimes objected to my dancing I shouted "People who have mattered much more to me than you couldn't stop me from dancing." I was living in constant conflict. For the sake of peace I thought of giving it up. For a couple of months I was like a dead body. I had no life in me. Then when I saw my guru I decided that was it— this was my life. It didn't occur to me that there could be any other life away from all this conflict, that I could live on my own, because it just wasn't done.

I always studied privately because I didn't start as a child, so I couldn't afford to wait for people. Training always started with the basic steps and basic movements, then gradually progressed to more difficult dances. When I studied Manipuri dance privately, the guru always came to my home. When I studied Bharatha Natyam I was so dedicated that I would get up at four in the morning and get into my class by five-thirty and study for three hours and then get back and get breakfast and all the other household things ready. Then I would go again in the afternoon and study while my husband was away at the office. I was happy in spite of all the conflicts because I was getting what I wanted and what I had been dreaming about all these years. My husband couldn't bear to see me being so happy so he asked for a transfer to take me away from Madras to Bombay, but that didn't stop me. In Bombay I found another guru and I started another style, Kathakali. I was swaying madly from one style to the other. Every dance form fascinated me— we have eight styles of classical dance. I just wanted to grab this and grab that. I was like a hungry person.

Kathakali was traditionally a man's form but I was one of the earliest women to take it up. It was developed in the Middle Ages, about the fifteenth century. It's traditionally story-telling with hand gestures, and like the Elizabethan drama it used to be done only by men with the female roles taken by young boys. It's very powerful, stylized acting with very stylized make-up. I studied that, but something was always missing. I couldn't find that complete total satisfaction until I came across Odissi.

Of all these styles, Odissi is the oldest, though it wasn't rediscovered till the fifties. I know the Odissi tradition that is special to the Devadasis, the temple dances. It used to be performed as part of a ritual. The Devadasis never regarded dance as art, it was always ritual for them. You danced to please the gods. Just as if you have been to a Hindu temple, you know that the deity is regarded as a very honoured guest. You wash his feet, you feed him, put beautiful flowers and clothes on him. You garland him and then you sing and dance before him in order to please him. The ritual revolved around the act of pleasing the deity. In the seventeenth century, the Muslims came and they vandalized the temples. Wherever they saw these beautiful young women dancing they got hold of them and defiled them so they could not go back to the temple and continue their work. Then the king decreed that this dance should be taught to young boys from ages seven to fourteen, before they sprouted a mustache, because boys stood in no danger of having their bodies defiled. At the beginning of this century, dancing in temples was banned. There was a law passed against it, partly due to the British who thought it was akin to prostitution. What could these temple dancers do when they were not allowed to go back to the temples? They had nothing else. So they sold their bodies and became mistresses of the local noblemen. Somehow the whole art fell into disrepute because of this.

The temple dancers were educated in the arts. They had to learn Sanskrit and the literature of the country. They were more educated in some ways than the housewives, like the geishas in Japan. Mothers would pass it on to their adopted daughters because they were not supposed to marry. They would often choose a particularly talented daughter from a local family and bring her up as a daughter. In the early days it was considered a great honour to be consecrated to the temple. Even princesses would want to do that.

In the early days the temple looked after a dancer. When she was serving the temple, she was given a little place of her own, a house with a plot of land and enough food from the temple. Later the ruler decreed that the temple dancers could marry people from the temple so that they would have a man to look after them. They were allowed to marry the priests of the temple or anyone connected to the ceremony of the temple. For example, my guru's mother was a temple dancer married to a priest of the temple; he was from direct lineage.

After the turn of the century, dancers were not allowed to dance, but they were allowed to sing. Singing is still going on at the temple. In the forties, when there was no income coming from the temple, my guru took the art of his ancestors outside the temple. He joined a sort of theatre troupe and started teaching people.

I know that dance now can mean anything— it can be film dance, night-club dance; it can also mean classical dance. That's why I am so particular about calling us classical dancers. I don't want people to confuse me with the cheap kind of cabaret dancing or night-club dancing that goes on in the name of dance.

I toured a lot and had been to Europe many times by the time I came to this country in 1968. Ted Shawn was corresponding with me and asked me to come over but he couldn't give me passage. I wanted to come but couldn't organize the fares for myself and my musicians. In the meantime, I got an invitation to Russia while I was touring Europe. I did that and it was very successful and they gave me a lot of money. On the last day, as I was leaving, they told me I couldn't take the money out of the country, but we could spend it in their shops. We had to catch a plane and had little time so we went through all the department stores where I bought tape recorders and cameras like mad. At least I could use the money to set up a little business or something. The moment I came to India the customs people grabbed all of my hard-earned money transferred into goods. So the next time, a year later, when I got the invitation from Russia I suddenly had this idea. Why can't I use the money they pay me on their airline and get to America? Surprisingly enough, they agreed, so the money was just enough for three musicians, my son, and myself. We came to America on Russian money. Then we came back to Russia because we had round-trip tickets and it was their job to send us back to India. It was wonderful.

My first engagement was at Jacob's Pillow. Ted Shawn's great idea was to have ballet, modern, and ethnic— three distinctive forms on the same program. That's why he was so devoted to ethnic dance. He himself was a great admirer of Indian dance forms as well as Spanish and other forms. Ted Shawn had a great vision. I was very close to him. He was very fond of me. Every time I wanted to plan a tour in America— which was every alternate year— I would combine it with Europe then come to America via Russia.

I didn't have an agent and organized all the tours myself. I corresponded with all the different societies in Europe, like the Swiss-Indian Society, the German-Indian Society. It was their duty to bring over Indian artists and I was very popular in those days. My father died very soon after I started touring so he just had a glimpse of the success I was getting. My mother was reconciled with it. The last few years of her life she was totally on my side.

In 1972, on the fourth tour, I met the person who was going to be the Chairman of the Dance Department at New York University. He invited me to come and teach dance. This coincided with the aftermath of my divorce. I had this little son to bring up— he was only ten years old at that time and my income in India was very uncertain. As a dancer I could never be sure of earning enough to keep the home fires burning, and this was a prestigious position, so I left India to come here. I wasn't really settled until 1974 or 1975. I was coming and going between the two countries and it was very strenuous. If I went to India to see my son, I would be very worried that my job would be taken away, and if I came here I kept pining for him. All this was settled in 1978 when my son came to me. My life had come full circle. Till then I had known only airports, madly going between one country and the other.

I say very openly, very proudly that I never really loved any man as much as I loved dance. If dance were to take the form of a man tomorrow then I would certainly embrace that person. I never had any relationship as passionate as that. Only two things have really satisfied me: my dance and my relationship with my son. From dance I can get everything I could possibly want from a relationship, the same kind of joy and ecstasy, the same kind of pain, also. In a relationship you have to depend on the other person, but dance is all mine. To dance well or to dance badly depends on me and on my body, on how well I look after it, and how well it is attuned.

I don't any longer do things I learned from the guru in the past. I feel that I've done them, I gave so many years to them, and I've tried to do them as faithfully as I was taught. So much of me has gone into these dances, very much beyond what my guru taught me. How can my guru, as a man, ever understand the feelings of a woman? When I'm portraying the role of a woman, so much of me has gone into it which no guru could ever teach me. I specialized in the stories of women, especially the five women whose stories I was the first to dance altogether.

These are all five legendary characters. They all suffered in some way or other. I started dancing the stories of women in 1971, when I presented them all together with great difficulty. He wasn't willing to part with them. Indian gurus are a sort of breed by themselves. They are almost unwilling to part with their treasures. They give you just a little bit at a time. They leave you hungry for more. It took me six years to recover all the five dances, but finally it was a great day for me when I danced them all together in a three-and-a-half hour concert in Bombay. That was my special contribution to the revival of Indian dance. And then of course, this remained with me— this desire to speak for women who were not to able speak for themselves. If I've survived at all it's entirely due to two things: my love for my son and my love for dance.

Basically my themes are taken from Sanskrit literature. There are so many beautiful works in Sanskrit that fascinated me from an early age, and in the last few years I found this music composer in Orissa who composes music for me. This costs me a lot of money, but then I don't splurge on anything else! So every year I go to Orissa. I give him the themes and he composes the music for it. For me it is much more of a joy to dance my own work than to dance somebody else's compositions. I've done that in a part of my life but I am not a parrot. I have my own ideas that are just dying to be brought into the light.

I think that people in present times have become very inhibited. Take the miniature sculptures, for instance. They emphasize the line of the body, the voluptuous curves of the body. All of these are very important in our dance. We're not straight, like in modern dance, or even in ballet with unusually long extensions. In our dance it is always the S shape of the body, what we call *tribhanga* or thrice bent— head on one side, hip on the same side, and the torso opposite. Therefore it is very important to have a waistline, to have a clear separation of the bust from the hips, and then, of course, the costume is supposed to show the lines of the body to its best advantage. The costume is not transparent and what we wear is usually thick silks.

I have tried my best to maintain the lines and since I'm a small person the only way I can show the line properly is to do without the covering of the bust, which most Indian dancers wear. I have been criticized for this so often that it's not worth it for me to continue wearing that kind of costume any more. These days I wear something that is transparent. It satisfies the purists and it satisfies me in the way of line.

I wouldn't advise Odissi for men because the male body doesn't have these curves. How can a man have that kind of hip, that kind of bust, in order to bring out these curves? Even children— I flatly refuse to teach children Odissi until they develop curves. They can't take those beautiful poses.

In the temple dance tradition, the expressions on the face are very feminine. Even the expressive acting varies from style to style. I was first attracted to it by the beauty of the line and the grace and femininity. The stories came much later, because I had no idea that these stories were there till I had contact with my guru. Then gradually, through conversation, I came to realize that these were there and I kept on begging him, cajoling him to give them to me. It just depends on what your body wants— your body falls into place when it finds the right style. You can experiment with different styles but only one style feels right and then you sink into it and there is no foreign feeling at all. That's why, when I get students, for instance, I have to look at them first before I can decide what is good for them style-wise.

I belong to the second batch of dance pioneers and we had the passion and the charisma. That's what kept us going. You realize how much you value something only when you struggle for it. Now, dance is going to the wrong people, sometimes the mothers are frustrated dancers. They couldn't dance in their adolescence so they want to push it down the throats of their own children. I have the fate of teaching these reluctant children. I have even offered to teach the mothers. Regardless of your age or your size you learn it, just to satisfy your own thwarted instincts. And they haven't taken me up on it. They're afraid of what their husbands will say, what society will say, even here. That is the same situation more or less in India, except that there the children have no choice. They have to learn what is available. At the most, they look forward to getting into a nice costume and standing on a stage and maybe attracting a young man who would eventually propose marriage. That is what dance has become— a passport to marriage. And then, because it deals so much with the body, it has been taken by the movie people. Now every actress who has the slightest potential towards dancing learns something and performs on the stage. In this country, you never see a movie star coming on the stage and performing a dance or a ballerina going on the screen. But in India, the lines are broken down. You have the actresses coming out to the public platforms and grabbing performances we classical dancers would be dying for. And getting more money than we could ever hope to get ourselves. In India the future is bleak for the classical dancer who is unfortunate enough to have stuck to her art and who is probably not as glamorous as a movie star and cannot command popular admiration.

All dance is sacred to me. Dance is religion. At my performances the program always mentions that dance is my religion. Now what you see in India is a galaxy of dancers who look the same, dress the same, dance the same, almost as if they were churned out by a machine. They're all brilliantly trained because they've all started out as children— the kind of luck we didn't have. Their technique is remarkable and dazzling, but they all look the same and none of them has the kind of passion that can uplift the dancer as well as the audience. It's only when you feel emotions deeply yourself that you can stir your audience and share with them.

To appreciate a thing, you have to suffer for it. You can feel to a certain extent, but when you are afraid of losing it, when you're afraid of not getting it at all, true love for it comes out. There had been so many points in my life when I was about to lose this very precious thing. That is why I clung to it with all my strength. In India, audiences don't appreciate older women who dance because every day there are younger girls coming up. The question, though, is how much can they show? And what can those who have no experience of life show in their acting? Maturity only comes when you have gone through certain experiences in life. Then you can bring tears into the eyes of your audience. One doesn't have to have all the experiences. One doesn't have to die to show death on the stage, but with that exception the more mature you are the deeper your acting is, and acting is the soul of Indian dance. Technique is just the pre-work. What you call the abstract dance is there, but you go beyond it when you go into the region of acting which is unique to Indian dance. It is then that you really bring out the soul of the dance, of the art. And you can't get that at an early age. You have to live through certain emotions and experiences in order to really portray those emotions properly. Unfortunately, just as dancers are maturing into that phase of their life, the audience wants to write them off. That's not the case with musicians. Musicians can go on performing. Ravi Shankar filled Carnegie Hall when he was seventy-two. Can you imagine a seventy-two-year-old dancer on stage? We are wrapped up with the idea of youth, beauty, and the body. The body is just the framework. If you are beautiful inside, the body becomes beautiful automatically. You notice it. A certain amount of looking after it is needed. I do feel that a dancer should treat her body just as a musician would treat his instrument. Nobody would play on a defective instrument and produce great music and a dancer can't allow her body to just go to pot and expect to produce great dance out of it. You've got to look out for your body. That's your instrument, but the music you produce from it, that is a matter of soul. If your soul is not mature then you can't really bring out those kind of nuances.

For me, Odissi is an expression of the female soul. It is a combination of strength and grace. A woman is really basically strong even if people don't think of it that way. The kind of suffering a woman goes through is sometimes more than a man can take. You've seen so many men taking to alcohol when faced with a life situation that they can't handle. They go and drown themselves in drink. How many women do that? Not many in India, anyway. They just have to grit their teeth and beat whatever calamity falls their way. So mentally women are strong and physically they are strong because I think the pain of bearing a child is very intense and very few men would be able to go through that pain. Women have that strength in them and at the same time they have the grace. I'm talking about the ideal, not just anybody. They have the grace to temper that strength, to know when to endure, when to exert their strength, and when to surrender.

The way I used to dance before is not the same as the way I dance now. We live and learn and the only way I can translate my life experiences is by dancing them. Whenever I wanted to say something to a special person or to an audience, I have always done it through dance. You have that expression, "say it with flowers," well, I say it with my dance. Mine is not a mass appeal art. I can't hope to fill Madison Square Garden, for instance. The handful of people who come to my performances— and those who go away with a feeling of fullness and upliftment— are those rare people who do appreciate what I do. And I am happy with that.

RINA SINGHA

Rina Singha is a teacher and performer of Kathak dance, a tradition of classical Indian dance that formed a part of temple celebration and entertainment in the royal courts of India. Rina trained and performed professionally in India before moving to England where she pursued her career as a solo artist. She later moved to Canada and has made Toronto her home. In addition to teaching, choreographing, and performing, Rina co-authored a book, Indian Dances: Their History and Growth, *documenting the history and growth of classical Indian dance. Rina is a strong believer in the value of dance. "People need to dance and I believe that everybody can," she said. She is devoted to answering this need in herself and in others. We began our conversation with a brief look at the history of women in classical Indian dance.*

When you talk about the history of women in classical Indian dance, you have to talk about the different parts of India. It is a regional history that changes with the different conquerors and political systems. For example, in North India women did not dance except during the prehistoric Vedic period. Women must have been dancing then because the terra cottas of the Indus Valley civilization all show women dancers doing a stylized kind of dance. In the Vedic period, women had a very high place in society, but later, during the wars, women became more protected and sheltered. Then begins the period where men did the temple dances. Later, in the Batki cult, that is about the twelfth or thirteenth century, women danced again when mysticism in Hinduism appeared and the Krishna cult started. This is in relation to the religious ceremony. The history of secular dance in the courts is different again. When the moguls came to India, they established their court and brought with them several classes of dancers from Persia and elsewhere. These dancers learned the temple dances from India and combined Indian dance with their own dance styles to create the court style of dance done by the courtesans. These dancers learned the classical dance style and adapted the temple dances to the court style which was secular, not religious. This court style took over from the temple style which was not thought to be as classy or as sophisticated.

In South India, women were outlawed from dancing as temple dancers. The dancers were attached to the temple, but there were a lot of abuses of the system. Although they belonged to the temple, they were really used by the wealthy people of society. In some cases the women were available to everybody. In other cases there was a ritual in which they were married to the deity, but somebody else— a priest or a citizen— would perform the rites of the husband. Women who belonged to that caste of dancers were put down, yet in some cases they had a very high status in society. For one thing, because they were married to the deity they could never be widowed, which was a very bad position socially. Also, the dancers were called upon to perform at all important functions. They had a mixed status. In some cases they were considered auspicious, in other cases they were looked down upon. Within themselves they must have had a lot of problems dealing with being accepted and not accepted at the same time. I was reading an interview with one of the dancers who went through the system and was in the middle of the dance movement when it was outlawed. This beautiful artist just disappeared from sight. She secluded herself and lived in a hut when she was found and interviewed. As she was recounting these tales about her life, she talked about being accepted and not accepted at the same time. Obviously the dancers could not have been very happy with their lives. Dancers are thinking people and because of the type of dance they were doing they went through intensive training, philosophical as well as physical. They were not just learning exercises, they were expanding their minds, too. So at some point, with all the discord going on around them, with all the learned people around them, they had to be caught up in the dilemma of being thinking bright women who would be good company, but at the same time were not allowed the same status as a housewife. It was a tricky situation. Then Indian dance was outlawed in the thirties. It was outlawed because a lot of middle class, educated Indians petitioned against it and the British system supported this move. As a result, Odissi completely disappeared. Odissi is a completely reconstructed dance form because the dancers all disappeared. It was being reconstructed when I was in Delhi in the early fifties. The men, the musicians, not the dancers, began to reconstruct it from what they remembered of it. In Orissa the women couldn't dance at all. At least in South India they still kept dancing; in North India where they had aristocratic patrons the nautch dancers still kept dancing. But in Orissa it was completely outlawed. Women went to prison if they were found dancing. As a result, most of them became nurses, because nursing, like dancing, was considered to be a bad or low profession. It wasn't outlawed because society needed nurses, but it was looked down upon because the women were serving men and touching bodies. It was considered that if you were a nurse you had a very loose character; the same with dancers. In the fifties when I started dancing there was still a lot of social stigma attached to it. Now dancing is accepted as a profession and women can make a living at it, although to have a good job you have to struggle.

The training now is not as intensive as it was for us. When we were trained we had very distant goals. We didn't think in terms of performing and never mentioned it to our teachers. If they said we want you to do something then you did it, but you never ever mentioned that you might want to perform. That was not supposed to be your goal; eventually yes, but not at that moment. Your goal was to learn to do it properly, to get it right. Very often our teachers would say things like, if there is a beautiful flower in the forest, the flower doesn't have to go tell everybody, "Here I am, a beautiful flower." Whoever wants to see the flower will come to the forest to see it. Bees come to honey. The honey doesn't have to go running after the bees.

They used those kind of metaphors to say, learn to do a good job and you will get noticed. If you just want to get noticed then you are not going to do a good job because your goals have gotten mixed up. We believed that and never thought to question our teachers. It made sense to us because we saw them doing the same thing. All of them still practised all the time. They didn't stop working at it just because they were super artists. Also, there was no time limit; you didn't say that in six months you are going to become a brilliant artist. It was just whenever you are ready you will become a brilliant artist. You work at it and some will take longer, some will not. It didn't matter, it was all an individual effort. People in the class worked at their own pace and each one would arrive when they had mastered each thing as they went along.

The training is not as intensive now because these goals have shifted. People join a school for a five-year or a three-year or even a one-year program. It was unheard of for us to think of a one-year program. Now at the end of a year, people get a certificate. They pay their fees, they expect to learn a certain number of things on the syllabus. And there is a responsibility on the part of the institution to make sure that students learn these things by the end of the year. Then whether they have learned them very brilliantly or not they will still be moving ahead. Even the bigger institutions have had to do that because there is so much competition. We were also taught a lot of theory as we went along and we did research into our own art form. We didn't need to be told that. But now if you are into being competitive there isn't the time to do theory and practice. Whereas when we were training, the goal was not to shine in front of your fellow creatures so you could develop a more solid background. And then it wasn't reversed on you. You knew what to expect and you stayed in the program, working at it at your own pace. But I don't think that system works now because the teachers may not have the same goals. We were taught by people who were taught that way and at that point there wasn't any need to do it otherwise. Now the whole of society has changed. Everything is instant. Goals are instant.

You are judged by how many programs you get in a year, how many times you perform somewhere. Teaching for performance or teaching for learning are two different things. You can't work as intensively. You can't go at the same thing a hundred times when you have short term performance goals. What I mean is, you can't have short term goals. Everybody is learning to perform. You are not learning to go and dance in your own closet, so it's presumed that the people who are coming to learn are going to perform at some time or other, except for the rare person who doesn't. But there is a difference between short term performance goals and performing when you are really ready for it, when it is the expression of all that is inside you. If you are learning just for the sake of learning a short item then it's not really good enough because you can't go into the depth which is required. The dance has to stay with you; it has to become second nature and that takes time. You can't do that with short term performance goals.

I started to perform when I was fourteen. Six months after I started studying there was a competition in my school and all the students were in it. I came first in that competition although there were senior students with me. Our teacher used to make us dance from time to time and the school would put on projects, reviving old dances. But really we never thought in terms of performing. When I joined the professional company I was not very performance minded, and although I was given major roles I was very terrified of doing them because I didn't feel I had enough skills. I found the expression part very difficult, because I would get so uptight and that's all my body would show. My body was not going to relax and show anything I was supposed to. I had a very difficult time to begin with till I felt comfortable. I really wanted to get on with my dance classes and with my learning. I wasn't keen on being a performer at that stage of my life. Then when I went to England I started performing just by myself, developing my own style. I was a solo artist and I would take my suitcase and go to all kinds of little concert halls. That was my period of growing up. Then I really began to perform. Even now I like performing, but I also like teaching. I also like dancing for myself. Performing has never been an urgency in me. Maybe that's not good, but...

In performance I found that the giving came from being more comfortable with myself. All the time I was trying to convey consciously I had a problem with it. Then I started to relax after dancing for myself. In Canada, I used to dance for myself in my basement and I think that was good in a way because I was able to knock out of my system all those embarrassing things I would have done in front of an audience. I think I always danced more for self-fulfilment. I convey my thoughts but it is more like people are looking in on my mind or my heart or my being. Now I enjoy performing but it has maybe come about in a roundabout way. I do it when I have something to say and usually I am saying it to myself. That doesn't mean I ignore the audience but it is more for myself. I don't know what route other performers take. This is the way it has been for me because of the way my life is shaped and my own tendency to be reflective and philosophical. I am saying that now but I don't think I recognized it all these years. I do look at life in a very philosophical way with all the whys and wherefores and I think that is in my dance too. I love performing but if I am not performing it will not kill me. It will make me lazy. Deadlines make you stay on the ball a little.

The joy of dance should be shared by everybody and I really am a believer of that. I find that to be true whether I work with adults or children. Everyone wants to move to music, so it is very important that you don't pull them down by negative remarks but encourage them to move while working at skills. I am opposed to just letting them get up and do their own thing because that only makes everybody stand like a stiff pole. Even when I am doing creative work with children I always work their skills up to a certain level before I let them go and create. You can't create in a vacuum. And people are shy about their bodies. They think they are being awkward, so you have to quickly give them skills that make them feel they are moving gracefully. Then they will be comfortable enough to let go. If you do very difficult things with them then they feel so awkward they might never try it again. But I think the world would be a happier place if everybody danced. People would not be so tense and the time it takes to dance would be that much more time away from their negative feelings and thinking.

People need to dance and I believe that everybody can. But performing and dancing for your own pleasure are different levels of dance and each has to be recognized as important. It is not that performers are above the others. You should be able to allow that I might want to perform, but that doesn't mean everybody wants to or has to or has to have their skills refined to that level. But still, people cannot feel good about themselves if they are just moving clumsily. They need some skills; otherwise it is self-defeating. You have to help people feel that they are moving gracefully and that there is some point to what they are doing. You can't water it down and water it down until it has no shape at all. Then what is the point? You might as well go to another activity. People want the discipline. They don't want to be molly-coddled. You've got to encourage, but at the same time challenge and keep a variety of activities with goals in mind. Each lesson should have an individual level of achievement that you are aiming at. You have to plan lessons. Just because it is dance doesn't mean you can do otherwise. Better give it some thought. Ask, where was I last time? Where am I taking them? You see, this is respecting the individual and believing that where you are taking them matters. If it doesn't matter to you it is not going to matter to the student. Everything requires discipline and training and yet everything can be enjoyed by all— all the art activities.

My work in schools is very different. It is more overall child development and curriculum learning. But I am very much concerned about children learning to be equipped as human beings, that they look at themselves and how they are with others. I try to introduce them to a different way of doing things through an artistic perspective. Kathak is more solo work; in the schools I do more group work which shows them, in a practical way, that they have to get on with each other. A group dance falls apart if two people are pulling in opposite directions or are fighting one another. If you show them that it just doesn't work, then the children clarify it on their own. By their actions they see there may be a better way of doing things. It may be better if we smile at each other, hold hands and work at a problem together. That kind of thing will go on forever and I know it may be just a small drop in the ocean, but to me it is important. I am not telling them that that is the only way. I am just introducing them to it. It is such a competitive world for them that it is important to bring this kind of calmness into their lives, for them to have fun and enjoy each other, while of course they are improving their dance skills.

I have never ever wanted to give dance up, not when I was training. I did give up the professional company because, in the beginning, various aspects were not to my liking. I got off to a wrong start. Afterwards, when I knew everybody in the company, it was fun, but it wasn't getting you anywhere like the classes. With the classes, even though you didn't learn something new every day, the overall development of your work was going on all the time and that was good. And it was really something to be taught and watched over by such great artists and teachers. We were taught very well, with great care and great love.

For me the hardest thing about dance is to keep on practising: self-discipline. It's so easy to give up, to say I don't want to practise today. That's partly because I am doing so many things. Your mind goes from one thing to the next. You get tired mentally and then you don't want to get up and dance. But you have to haul yourself up and start working again. Once I get going, then I can keep going for hours, but that initial pulling in is the hardest thing.

All my work is my own choreography; all my solo works are my own. Way back I did several short pieces based on Indian miniature paintings— *Moods of Women*; then I did a piece called *Interplay*, isolating movements from Kathak for black light. *Genesis* I did as a mixed media piece. It was the story of the creation and was very successful. Some people think it is my best work so far. For the International Year of

Women I did *Indian Women,* a mixed media piece showing different stages of a woman's life, starting from childhood.

Sometimes I find it difficult to choreograph. Sometimes I get bogged down with one movement; it keeps coming back and I don't know why. Other times I establish one movement as a key movement and I need to repeat it at intervals to establish it as the main motif for the piece. You've got to take many things into account. Some days it comes and some days you keep at it and then suddenly it happens. When I choreograph I get burdened with something I want to say. I get an idea in my head. Then I go to India where I have a music director who does the music for me. At that point I only have a tentative plan for my dance. I don't work very well in India. There are no mirrors and I get intimidated by the scene there because I am doing things that are a bit extreme for them. And they haven't watched my development, so they really don't understand what I am doing. I am more comfortable doing my work here. My music is the most expensive part. I get a tape that I invariably have to edit when I get back here.

Being a dancer is hard work. Physically it is very demanding and the discipline is hard. I think it would be easier if I only performed or if I had a dance studio or a company on a regular basis. But when you've got to do other things and then fit dance in it becomes hard. At least two or three months a year I do only Kathak, then I have to get off it and get on with earning a living. Also, you really do need somebody to take care of the business part. Anyway I still manage. I often think it would be more effective, that I would be able to go further ahead, if I had someone to do that. At the same time, you've got to get somebody you can really trust and work well with, but by the time you find that person you might as well get on with what you're doing. It takes time to build a team.

Dancing is not the best paid profession so dancers have to get on with the business of earning a living to give them the independence to do what they really want to do. Because you want that independence you are going this route, but it doesn't leave you time to be actively involved in a lot of things even though you could support them in other ways. That's why I haven't been part of the women's community very much because I am usually busy earning a living or doing my other work. But I'm very involved with women's issues just because I am a woman and have been an immigrant woman. I know all the heartaches and problems so I really identify with the women's movement.

My work is demanding but I enjoy it. Every day I know I've arrived somewhere: I've taken somebody forward somewhere and helped some person out. I don't mean to sound like a do-gooder type, but it is fulfilling to know that you are able to help somebody see things in a different light and reach into themselves a little more. When I was younger I used to make a big joke about people who asked "Who am I?" Why do you need to know who you are? But I realize how fundamental that is. You have to be in touch with yourself and recognize that need as an important one and not negate it all the time. That takes a lot of doing for women because we are out giving, giving, giving. Everybody else is more important and you keep yourself in the background. You want to be nice and you don't want to make waves and there are children to care for. But then to find yourself again and recognize your need for yourself as important is a long way up and that is practically a full-time job. So you don't get the same kind of time to go out and do a lot of things you would want to.

I keep dancing because I want to dance and I have something to say. It took me a long time to recognize that for myself and to say it. I was given this gift at a high level of skills and I was let out into the world as a dancer, but I wouldn't call myself a dancer. I couldn't come right out and say I am a dancer and recognize that need. By dancer I mean an artist who expresses herself through dance. I could not get myself to say that, because it took me a long time to recognize that; in the same way that people paint pictures, I dance my ideas. I was not willing to recognize that in myself, even though the dance would be like a burden in my head that I had to get out. Now I say, all right, I'm going to do it. I only hope that people still like what I do and that I can keep doing it.

Once you are in it and trained you really can't get it out of your system. The need has remained in me. I could have been teaching in a university or high school, but what kept me from doing that must have been this need for dance. I wanted the freedom. So I didn't allow myself to get caught up in something, because some inner being said, "No, no, no, you've got to leave yourself free to dance." Even when I wasn't performing, I was researching dance, reading about dance, working with children in dance. I never got away from it. It's an interesting life and I think that is the way it is in so many fields. Everybody has something inside them. If we all could recognize that and not worry that it has to come out today, just work toward it once we recognize it.

ANAHI
GALANTE

When she was in her early thirties, Anahi Galante left her position as soloist with the Ballet del Sur in Argentina to study modern dance in New York. This shift gives Anahi a unique perspective on the differences between ballet and modern dance, and the role of women in each. Anahi brings a very conscious political perspective to her work. Her growing political consciousness during the dictatorship in Argentina made her uneasy with her role as a ballerina as she drew more and more parallels between fascism and ballet. Finally making a break with a form which she felt perpetuated alienating values, she moved to New York, where she began to train all over again, this time in modern dance. Changing her way of dancing, she says, changed her way of thinking.

I think there is a particular gestural language for men and women. I also believe that our psychology and our biological nature are so different, they make us different. I'm not saying this in a sexist way. I think gestures have to do with a particular psychological and physical self and that our way of expressing is different from men's.

Women's gestures are more gutsy and internal. We really use what comes from the abdomen and the guts. Everything about men is external. When I work with male dancers, and I ask them to get internal, they have a much shorter limit than a female dancer. A female dancer enjoys going in more than being external. A lot of that is socialized. We are following a social pattern. Part of it is what society makes us do, and the other is how much we believe in what society makes us do.

Ballet took me away from my own power and made me feel like a dumb blonde because it is so external and stereotypical. It stereotypes everything: reality, personalities, and situations. Modern dance technique helped me to go deeper and dig into who I am, why my body moves in the way it does, and why it can move in other ways.

I come from a fascist country, and I have experience living under a dictatorship. Ballet is very close to a military fascist system. It's a denial of the body, a denial of the opportunity to be yourself. The funny thing is, I was a good ballet dancer. I didn't quit because I couldn't form myself on toe shoes. I was a prima ballerina for many years. I started to study when I was seven, and I began dancing professionally when I was twelve. And on that day I also began to smoke. Ballet is such a denial of everything, that you become neurotic, while modern dance allows your body to do what your body needs. It has a more balanced point of view, and more respect for your nature. Ballet is connected to a stereotype of woman. They have to be thin, or have a certain breast and hip size. In modern dance, every size is allowed.

I remember saying, I want to dance, so my mom brought me to the neighbourhood flamenco school, and I said, No! Then she sent me to the folk dance school and I said, No! Finally someone told her about the classical ballet school in the Municipal Theatre so my mom brought me there and I said, Yeah! I don't know where I got the idea that ballet was dance yet I knew that ballet was the dance form I wanted. The other forms of dance didn't have that delicacy that is so important to me. It was a very strict school and my first year I went twice a week for dance technique and musical appreciation. In Argentina we were one hundred years behind Europe or the States, in terms of pedagogical methods. It was very very strict but I loved it just the same. It gave me the chance to prove my strength, and it was my moment. I didn't have to share it with my family. It was my own war.

The first time I really questioned dance, I was on a stage doing *Swan Lake*. I remember thinking, What am I doing here? What is this about? This has nothing to do with me. I was very political and concerned about social things. Ballet was politically incorrect because it was a reminder of our war, where there were many different and unequal lives. The whole structure with the soloist or prima ballerina and the corps in ballet is unequal. The corps de ballet doesn't dance— they stay there like the working class and their salary is lower but they do the hard work even if it doesn't show. Ballet was a celebration of a world I didn't support. I also wanted to dance for the working class, for the real people, for the people I was with whenever I wasn't at the ballet company doing my political work. I would talk to my political friends about ballet, and they said, "Well, what is that?" The first version, when you just start developing your leftist point of view is that the bourgeoisie have the theatre, and they have the monopoly of the arts. But, in fact it is the language that is problematic. Ballet doesn't allow us to recognize ourselves. Ballet doesn't work as a language because the technique and the aesthetics are holding a point of view from way back in history. Aesthetics evolve with real life. For instance, what do we pretend with toe shoes? That we look thinner and are floating? That's a denial. Even I have weight.

We tried to unionize the ballet company because we were not getting the salary or social security we should. It was ridiculous. The prima donna wanted something that was very different from what everybody else was asking for. We were just asking for basic things that would affect the quality of the dance. For example, we would send absolutely inadequate dancers for roles, just because they were prima donnas. Even though someone in the corps de ballet was great for a role they couldn't be used. I came from a very political family, and I have my own political way of thinking, which is very rare in a ballet dancer. Actually, I believe that's why I'm alive. The military and the police never thought that I was carrying guns on my back. A ballet dancer! Maybe that's why I'm alive. I was sensible to political and social causes so it was hard to hold a position in a ballet company.

After the day I found out I didn't want to have anything to do with ballet it took me twelve more years to break away. I was in a company with a salary, so it was great to make my living from dancing. I was making my living as a dancer but not from doing what I wanted to do with dance. There wasn't that much to learn from, so I had to explore.

I discovered improvisation, and I discovered that I was a great improviser. I went into theatre which allowed me to go deeper into what I wanted but I couldn't remember my improvisations. I didn't have an instructor to help me read movement that wasn't a combination of classical ballet and steps. That's why I came to New York. It took me a long time because I'm from a working class family, so I didn't have any money. It took me ten years to save enough money to come for a few months. In a way money was a big factor. It stopped me from coming earlier.

The first six months were a horrible struggle. I cried every day after class. After being a successful dancer it was horrible to be told I didn't know how to walk. What do you mean, I don't know how to walk? I've been walking for ten years on a stage. And one day I understood. I realized that I was an idiot with my body. I felt that I had been killing my sensitivity for many years with this strict training. A tendu wasn't about going on pointe. It was the experience of going out and coming in, how the rest of the body could be part of that experience, or how it could be isolated because there is an existentialist spatial reason for the movement. It was so hard to understand the concepts because I didn't speak English. When I finally was able to count in English it took me an extra second because I had to think that one is *uno* and *uno* is the first beat. That fraction of time was critical because I was always late. I'm proud that I stayed with it.

I felt a lot of honesty in that work. Suddenly I found myself thinking differently. One day I had a discussion with a friend in Argentina who said I changed my way of dance because I changed my way of thinking first. It is a switch to go from ballet into modern dance. But in fact, because I changed my dance language, I was able to change my system of thinking.

I experienced the existentialism of movement in a way that I never did before, the fact of using gravity or being heavy, for instance. If you dance, you really have to believe in it, you have to *be* heavy. For instance, one day I realized that a space doesn't exist unless you create it. Running the circle is *being* the circle, feeling that you are being pulled by the centre.

In a way I became my child again, everything was so new and intense. I was about thirty-two years old, which is old to change a whole system of life, to go from being a ballerina to having to clean toilets to pay tuition fees, and clean houses to pay rent. I was old for that type of life, and I wasn't used to it, yet I felt younger and younger and younger!

When I went back to Argentina I had to take ballet classes for three months because of my commitment to the ballet company. My body refused to do that. I just couldn't take the class. I was sad because I felt I was throwing away twenty-five years of work in my life. Of course, I decided I wouldn't think that way. I would think I was moving forward, and that change was a growing process. For the first time I felt like a dancer, not a ridiculous stereotype. Everything became more honest and more clear.

I felt hopeless politically in my country. It was so hard for me to recreate or to reinvent hope out of anything and I felt that the change I made in dance gave me the elements to keep in touch with my dear ones who disappeared, because I had a stronger way of connecting to them. It's the way we see energy. Energy is there because you create it as you move. I was able to catch them, and to catch their energy, because I was creating it. I *can* create this— this space is not there unless I create it— it gave me the chance of placing them and playing with them, going back to them, or allowing them to come to me. I reach so far out that sometimes I feel I can touch the soul of someone who has been disappeared for so many years. It was a magical experience to me even though I know there is nothing magical about the work, it's just working hard and understanding how the mechanics and dynamics work.

In ballet, my mind and body were divorced. There is no room to put them together because they're not connected. I don't think they're connected in ballet. If you are worrying about a class, you can still do the movement and after class you can do the dishes and go to the supermarket because there is no real connection. This is mechanical training and that's how I learned ballet. I learned how to give an order to my leg to go there and come back here, but it had to be a mechanical movement. I was not aware of integration. It's a real divorce, not an isolation and that's the difference. In modern dance, because we have this sense of unity or of a whole, we have the choice of isolating parts of our body if we have to or if we need to. In a way you have to be more connected than ever; otherwise, you really can't do the isolations. In modern dance you have a choice. In ballet, it's a fascist country. You don't have freedom, therefore you don't have choices. There isn't even a rational reason for it. When I talk like this, people, especially former ballet dancers, hate me. In a lecture–demonstration I did I talked about these things, and I went into an analysis of different steps. What is direction? I really don't think we have the sense of direction in ballet. We have the name of a position, but no sense of being frontward, sideward, backward, of releasing— all the different qualities of motion that make a complete being.

Ballet is the type of life men want women to have in our society. I believe this society is really run by men and they run it for themselves. Modern dance allows a kind of difference I believe in. I don't believe that we are equals. I believe and I fight for equal opportunities, but we are not the same. That also happens with modern dance techniques. You can do the same drop but you will do it one way and the male dancer next to you will drop differently. The female dancer next to you will also be different and still be herself. So there is room to be yourself, male or female, but there is a recognition of the uniqueness of your nature and your body, and definitely the recognition that you can build up an identity. In ballet denial is so important that you can't build up an identity. The fact that modern dance has more insight allows you to be yourself, discovering that everything is valid, every part of your body is important. And you can mobilize your body from wherever you want. I think modern dance is wider in every possible direction. It's wider not just in terms of space. It's wider in the body. My body got wider. My whole body changed.

I started to choreograph when I was very young. I had to. I think because of my political orientation I had to express myself. I needed to express my thoughts and it wasn't just about doing pretty dances. I started to choreograph when I was twelve and I was bossy, because that was the pattern I learned.

I came to New York because I really needed the technical support to be able to express what I wanted on stage. Ballet didn't work. I knew I had very good intentions, but I didn't have the knowledge to do it. So I came here to borrow knowledge from the masters. Because of these wider options, I was able to create the characterization of space that I thought was proper to what I wanted. Being on toe shoes, you are never on earth. Basically I had to find a way of getting down into the ground, to be rooted into the ground. I also had to find a way of being more honest. I had to find a way of offering those elements to my performers so we could make something believable. I got a greater sense of the use of space; this is important from an architectural point of view on stage. But what is most valuable to me is that I could find a texture or a tone to the character, and work with it to make it very different.

Now I am very clear about my dance language and my movement language as a choreographer. Now I have choices. If I use something it is because I want to, not because that's the only thing I know in order to move. Basically, *that's* the difference.

Dance is the only profession where we allow ourselves to speak with our bodies. Women are different from men and it seems that dancing is the only way society has allowed us to really be ourselves in our body. If you use your hips on the street, you are labelled. It's an important element. Also to express particular feelings, feelings of loss that women perceive. The first experience of loss a woman has is having a baby. You are having it, but you are losing it. Even with our period every month we lose something, and it's so important to us. A loss is a big deal for us and it twists our bodies. We go deeper into things. Of course, it's a generalization. Sometimes I see women who are bad propaganda for us. As a choreographer I see it, but sometimes my dancers don't understand what I'm talking about in terms of the body.

We really have a good sense, just from being women, of pain. And

I think that makes our gestural language different because it comes from a deeper place. It's very hard to have pain just on the surface. I always feel that pain is something very deep. Even if I have a cut on my finger, I don't have the feeling that the pain is on the surface. I have a feeling it comes from the middle of my finger. The central nervous system is very deep. Our whole language and the pain we're related with goes from in to out. If we have our period, the pain is right here in our belly. If you're giving birth, the pain is right here in our belly. If you are making love and we are not comfortable, we have pain here in our belly. So everything really happens here and helps us to go in. Once you are here, in order to go out, you have to make an extra step, an extra movement. You have to deliver more energy. That's how I distinguish the male language from the female language. Why do so many women consider pain a natural state? Women are the recipients of such physical violence. Why do we always have to receive it like this, instead of giving it back? In a way, I believe that because we are smaller we don't have the same type of physical strength to protect ourselves from attacks.

When I was a ballerina, I thought I had reached the end, that I was getting too old. I came to New York in a hurry, thinking, this is my last year. After I got all my training at the Nikolais school I went back to the fantasy that I could dance forever. Now I feel the years on my body. It doesn't scare me very much because I enjoy choreographing. If I have a good dancer who can represent what I want to express with my body I don't care if I'm not dancing. I'm going to miss it when I have to stop, because I really love dancing. I have to dance. I do everything with my body. Sometimes I feel maybe three more years; sometimes maybe ten more years. I keep digging into different ways of expressing motion and movement, so when it's not about a test of how I'm going to lift my leg, I think I can just keep going.

MAUREEN FLEMING

After interviewing Maureen Fleming, I observed her teaching a workshop. Using images of mud, water, smoke, and wind Maureen brought the participants through a series of movements motivated by imagery. It was like watching the miracle of movement. The imagery brought its own logic to the body and limbs floated effortlessly into space. Her own performances convey this quality of ethereal movement as she slowly unfolds her body into a series of astounding shapes.

Maureen Fleming works within a form which has been characterized as both stark and shocking. Butoh, she explains, began in post-World War II Japan as a political movement more than a dance movement. After years of training with Butoh masters in Japan, Fleming created her own brand of Butoh, transforming this post-war movement into a kind of feminine identity quest.

Butoh was initially created by Tatsumi, and it was a search for a Japanese identity after the war, asking "Who are we? What have we done? What does it mean to be Japanese?" And I think that what was happening was the answer, "We have nothing, we are nothing." They were throwing away incredible traditions associated with Japanese culture, the Samurai tradition and the connection with nature. Butoh was more of a political movement than a dance movement. It was a real revolution.

The dance is such a cry, a search for an identity, that one can stand behind. It came from questioning what is valid, asking what principles are really worth standing behind. It is a very shocking way of talking about particular realities, but I also feel that it is a statement about what man is doing to nature. It has became much more about the search for the transformative experience rather than something that is about the experience. When I look at modern dance, I see it as very beautiful in many ways, but it is not the experience itself. Martha Graham studied Indian rituals in New Mexico and created a dance about those rituals. She didn't create the ritual in her performances, while Butoh is a search to return to the experience, rather than an expression of the experience. That is what really fascinated me about it.

My father was in the military after the war and I was born in Japan. We moved from Japan when I was three years old, but I think the fact that I was born and conceived there was important. My teacher, Kazuo Ohno, also lives in Yokohama, the city I was born in. There is some kind of psychic connection.

I was trained in ballet. I had a seven year scholarship with Margaret Craske, who is the eighty-six-year old master of Cecchetti in New York. Ballet has very different kinds of technique. The Bournonville and Cecchetti techniques are very, very different, mainly in alignment. In Cecchetti, the alignment is slightly forward and this is similar to Aikido. That slightly tipped forward alignment is also the basis of Zazen. It employs the lower chakras in a way that is different from when you're straight up and down like what Balanchine has established. I found a connection between Butoh and Cecchetti mainly with the chakras, the energy centres in the body. A lot of the imagery in Butoh works at opening those chakras. I think that when those centres are opened, there is a real experience of transformation in the body that is not anything about the experience but actually is that experience. You feel psychically different. You feel emotionally different and it's a kind of catharsis, too. In order to get to that place, you have to wear a kind of an armour, and I think that Cecchetti is in that league. The flourishes of the hand and the softness of the body connect to the energy opening from the chakras.

Margaret Craske spent a lot of time in India, which is very strange for a ballet teacher. She taught in such a way that ballet did open up centres of the body. I felt very fortunate to have had that experience. Also there's something about being old— she was eighty-six, Kazuo

Ohno was eighty-six, when I studied with him— all those years of being devoted to movement must teach you something special. In my work I see a very similar understanding, although opposite to ballet's "turned outness" and its idea of trying to ascend and control nature. The opposite of that is true with Butoh, which is about wanting to go back to the ground, but I think that the kind of energy used inside is similar. There is a similarity between Cecchetti and, especially Kazuo Ohno's version of Butoh.

My first experience of Butoh was as a performer. I was hired as a dancer in a production of *Mythos Oedipus* by Min Tanaka. I was totally fascinated by Min Tanaka's movement. He would enter the room and I would feel different, my body would feel different and that fascinated me. Also the whole approach of movement from the imagination. Movement in Butoh is created by imagery. For example, you have the ocean moving up inside your body. If you think that thought, your body feels different— there is a lightness that comes inside your body from that feeling. If I were to sit here for fifteen minutes and think only that, I would feel very, very different.

The whole paradox is that you can't think a thought through your head. You have to get the head into the body. By just "thinking the thought," you may have the illusion that this is happening, but anybody watching you realizes that it's not.

The process is basically one of getting the breath into the body. As we grow older, especially in this society, people generally start to breathe only in their chests. If you watch a baby or an animal breathe, the breath is in the body. When you're not thinking about it at all, your breath happens in your body. If you're going to really unite the breath with the body, you have to go through some physical training. I think that when we had to walk or run a lot, and carry things on our heads as part of daily life, people were much closer to that. But now, as machines are doing more and more work for us, a time will come when every person will have to have a ritual to make that a reality. I think that any kind of genius is associated with that interconnection. In taking very simple movements, like jumping from one side of the room to the other, or combining that with basic Shiatsu, the breath goes into the body as an experience without thinking about it. It doesn't happen by thinking, "I'm thinking and I'm trying to make my breath go there." What are physical experiences? If you're thrown into a pool, you don't think about, "How can I get my breath down?" It just goes there, or you die, you freeze and drown. So I think that it's important to create experiences that give people the experience without thinking at all. In going through those activities you are going to be able to have an image and manifest it in the body.

Min Tanaka's idea is to push the body to its complete limit through exhaustion. He believes that the chaos created at that point of exhaustion and the irrational space that you get into is the beginning point of dancing. That's also very much in his life-style; he loves alcohol. For many shamans it's a very popular idea— breaking the body down through exhaustion. And I went through that.

In training we got up at eight in the morning and the first thing we did was to begin jumping. It's very extreme. Jumping and lowering the centre as much as possible and getting as wide a stance as possible, taking no care with alignment. Butoh camp— it's like boot camp. Go! Go! Go! And after you can't stand up any more, there are more exercises. Somebody runs around with a pillow and you try to hit the pillow with your knee or you slap each other's backs. It gets violent even, because if you don't get up quickly enough to slap the other guy's back, he starts beating you up. It's this kind of extreme place that he finds as a way to get in touch with this kind of energy. I was really very into that when I was working with him, until I got injured. It wasn't anything that happened in class. From all of the pounding of the body on the floor, I had a pinched nerve in my neck, and it just closed in. After a period of time the shoulder blades started dislocating from my back and the serratus muscle got paralyzed. I went to many doctors. I said, "You know, I lift my arm and it just hangs. It just wings out in the back." They said, "Well, it's a pinched nerve, and if you continue this kind of training, you're going to lose your eyesight and your entire arm will become paralyzed."

At the time they said, "We recommend that you stop dancing because it's become arthritic." When I heard that I was very traumatized. I went back to Japan because I had continued Min's training here in New York and I said, "Min, look what's happening to my body." He said, "Oh, just ignore it. I'm sure it will pass." Meanwhile, the doctors were saying, "If you continue, you're really going to mess yourself up." So it was really a great thing to have happen because when I got to this place, I realized that I had to think for myself. I quit the training and came back to New York and very slowly, through a diligent practice of Chinese healing, reading, and exercises I created my own technique. This technique came through a process of healing my body so I could dance. It has evolved over many years, and it's a combination of movements that deeply put the breath in the body with a very strong care for alignment and images that separate the spine. Later, when I worked with Kazuo Ohno, I found that most of his imagery is based in that kind of work, in images that lengthen the spine. One of his favourite images is the flower, where our body becomes a flower. The stem is growing very, very slowly. The flower is opening in the face and in the chest, which is the very chakra I was talking about. The arms are the leaves growing and the legs are the roots growing down to the centre of the earth. It's like the ocean moving up through the body. That image itself creates a certain kind of experience in the body. It's these kind of images that I have taken as the foundation of what I'm doing because they are images that create an experience of releasing and opening in the body.

Kazuo Ohno has no physical training at all in his work. He does not have a dance company, nor is he interested in actually making dances. It's really research for his own work and it's his way of sharing and having a community around him. I think it's a very positive thing but it's not really a training method for other people.

In my own workshops, I first start out by talking about a river in the body that has developed logs we are not aware of. As much as possible, we want to release the logs wherever they are and begin to recognize the experience of when they're released and when they are not. That's the first level— gaining that kind of awareness. I use self-massage to give people that experience. And I work with imagery that, as much as possible, puts the breath into the body so that people can start to experience the inner body opening up. Once that is really experienced strongly, we take the body into movement across the floor. In the initial part of the class I take great care in terms of alignment, but when I get into the imagery work, I'm really interested in exploring the limits of the body. I'm interested in finding the limitations of what the body can do through imagery and not just basing it in everyday movement which is what Kazuo Ohno worked in. Min Tanaka was more interested in pushing the body physically, like an athlete pushes the body. But I'm much more interested in making the body almost unrecognizable as a body, to make it a kind of transformation and a link between being a body and being a tree, for example. I'm also very interested in bringing together parts of my dance technique. By that I mean that when we talk about this river in the body, it is like the principle of Shiatsu, where you press and you stop the river for a moment and then you let it go and it flows more strongly. And so I began to discover that the same principle applies to twisting bodies. If you twist the body in a very extreme way, it's like cutting off that river for a moment. And then when that starts to release, you feel once again a heightened flow inside the body, so that it can become a very regenerative experience. I've also become very interested in surrealistic painting, the image of the crutch, for example, from Salvador Dali's paintings. If I imagine that I feel those crutches inside my body, with angels pulling the strings in different directions, a kind of movement starts to happen. Those images act as movement keys that set off a kind of dance that comes from a very deep part of the unconscious. And I think that like in certain religious traditions, for example, Voodoo, they begin to characterize possessions. What I've found through surrealist painting and certain images that have come to me is that these possessions can actually be created. For example, the pulling of the elastics. First you pull the elastic between the chin and tail-bone and then you pull it to the extreme, and then you begin to imagine being inside a glass ball and touching the edge of the glass ball to slowly reverse the current. A lot of times you get to the image of a moving snake figure or something like the ocean moving up in the body. I began to get interested in images that create these states, in periods of very, very strong breathing in the body and also places where you do movements without thinking when the breath does go into the body. If you follow the experience with imagery it becomes very ritualistic and releasing for people.

The next piece I'm going to work on is called *Evolution.* I want to create a series of rites of passage that characterize these different states, because I think that's one of the things missing in society. I think that's why we have so much of a drug problem. In our daily lives, we don't have rituals that take us into these very needed places of human experience. That is evolution. A guru in India said that drugs are the McDonald's of the spiritual world. I think that, as Americans, we have bought into that. We're not going to get over that by getting a stronger police force. It's only when the need for ritual is replaced with something more authentic that it's going to happen. So in my lifetime, I want to see programs in schools to help children create these rituals for themselves. I've been working for years for young audiences and I think it's unfortunate the way the arts are brought into education through the idea that "everyone is entitled to it." They don't want to have competitions and I think that's a big mistake. I think American Indians really understand how to bring art into a society by their powwows. They have a cash prize for the best dancer. I'm working on a proposal where I would go to a school and give a basic workshop to all the teachers with a group of children who would demonstrate these structured improvisations as part of their daily routine. It improves concentration, gets rid of stress and excess energy. Later, those students would go back to each class and be the demonstrators, so that the teacher would create a performance based on the structured improvisations learned at the beginning of the year. And then at the end of the year, all of the classes would perform their pieces in a dance festival and there would be a cash prize. They would compete. I really think that unless meaningful rituals for kids are created we will lose a wealth of creativity. I don't really like what Jacques d'Amboise does when he teaches ballet to children, because he has children imitate adult movement. Children's movement is so profound. It's much more profound than children imitating adult movement.

I now have a program called *Myth of Dance,* where we do space creatures and introduce dance to children in that way. It ends with a structured improvisation of children playing in the rain, and they join us in the last piece called *Rain Gatherers.* There's only one school who would listen to my ideas for implementing dance in the schools. That was Lake Country School, and we did a wonderful presentation at the Walker Arts Centre in Minneapolis. It takes a lot of commitment from parents. It means making the arts the focus of a particular year, and in that situation it was very high profile because it was done at the Walker Arts Centre. The people were willing to put their energy into it. That's what Jacques d'Amboise has done with his performances at Lincoln Centre. But unfortunately, their whole thrust is art for everyone, and they are really against any kind of singling out. I'm sure I can take a group of kids and do a fairly interesting performance, but when you have the opportunity to take the kids who are very interested, you can bring it to a completely other level.

Children have a natural organic balance. It's there in a very formed way outside of classical ballet. They have a natural connection to centre, especially babies. In every group of ten-year-olds, there are ten in two hundred who have that absolute understanding. If you could set up a situation where those children became the teachers in the class, you would have the creation of authentic ritual. I do a very simple exercise of following your hand with a string on your fingers. Then I put on Bach and tell the children to stop at a particular moment, always focusing on the hand. From that exercise alone, I can pick the ten children out of the two hundred who have a natural gift for dance. I once saw a kid throw his arm around, following the string leading his hand, and I saw him do five pirouettes without any training. That kind of natural genius exists, and we could create rituals to bring it out.

Ever since I could walk, I was choreographing and teaching dance to my sisters. I come from a family of nine children. We would put on *Snow White* and I was always the choreographer and I always made myself the lead dancer. I began ballet when I was very young. I was in the *Nutcracker* at a young age, and they created a part for me. In the part where one of the dolls falls down, they had me come on with a key to wind her up. I remember going on stage with the key, ready to wind her up, but I just paused. I must have stopped for three minutes. I just stood there in arabesque. No one knew why. I don't think I knew why, and then I continued. I was thinking about when I started Butoh and when I started moving slowly and I realized I always did it. For some reason, it was in me before I studied. Studying was more a way of recognizing and deepening my work with masters and people to refine what I already knew.

I think it's true that there is a way to get to our creative part without destruction. I'm interested in evolution. What is that? What is the evolution of humanity at this time? When you go to the Museum of Natural History, you see that we've been somewhere else; but where are we going? I think that the change of alignment, the ears going upward, the forward alignment of the face— all that relates to taking sexual energy and somehow taking that energy up to the brain. I think that is related to evolution. I said that I think that certain rituals will become a part of everybody's daily routine, like drinking coffee. The whole health club thing that has started across America is a part of that. Unfortunately, that exercises the outer muscles of the body, and that is not where the superior intelligence lies. I think it's in the deepest layers of muscles in the body. The more advanced exercise is going to be a way of working that part of the body. That has to do with alignment and getting breath to those places and also just recognizing that that's the objective of what we're trying to touch, the movement of the ligaments.

We certainly can't lift the legs any higher. It's more about finding an advanced kind of movement that doesn't necessarily have to do with moving away from the natural movement of the body.

The most important thing is that no matter what ability you have, you have the ability to transform it. For example, I've seen the American Indian Sun dance where they pierce the body and hang from the trees until they drop. That's an incredibly violent ritual, but the attitude about it is that they're doing it for their society. They are inflicting this pain upon themselves as a choice, as a way of giving to society. What's interesting is their attitude. Many people talk about this place where the body turns off and you don't feel pain, like in childbirth. What's interesting is to challenge yourself, not necessarily to move the pain but to try to understand the pain and use the ability to transform it.

I think that sometimes we experience a breaking pain and then we ignore it. We want to cut ourselves from it. That is bad pain and now I have to go somewhere else. I don't think it's that simple. I think it's about understanding why that pain was given to you and understanding the transformation. When you cut yourself off from pain, you run; you don't go to that next level, whatever it is.

There are certain times when I'm trying to be very feminine and there are times when I'm trying to define archetypes. There are certain feminine archetypes I try to communicate. And then there are other times when I want my body to completely transform itself into a very masculine archetype. There are other times when I really like to confuse people, so that there is absolutely no gender involved. For example, if I'm a tree it's just simply a tree. I think I'm very conscious of what archetype I'm trying to create at a particular time. I ask for a lot of feedback from people. I'll ask a cab driver, "What do you see?" and I find that very important research. I really want to make dances for the person who is watching. I don't want to make dances that are my therapy. I want my dances to communicate.

My body is basically very feminine and I have created choreography that brings that out. My choreography doesn't try to disguise that. To tell the truth, I couldn't fit my body into the mould of the Balanchine look. I have created an acceptance of the female body through my choreography as a way to actually dance with a very female body.

Kazuo Ohno, my mentor and teacher, is eighty-six, so I don't have the feeling that I'm getting old and I can't dance. But I think sometimes that I'm getting older and I don't have the flexibility my choreography demands. Yet I'm finding that as I get older I get more flexible and that's really surprising. I don't know how it's going to go because certainly if I can't create my shapes I don't want to dance. Of course I will always create dances, but I'm not interested in working with dancers if I cannot pay them, because my work is too demanding, and I'm not interested in dancing unless it can be as demanding as it is.

I'm really looking for a ritual where the end result isn't martial, but creative. That's what Butoh is at its best. In its foundation, Butoh wanted to work in everyday movement. I'm interested in using some of the very same principles, but expanding into movement that acknowledges that whole heavenly body and movement that is not cut off from the natural shape of woman.

SARA
PEARSON

Sara Pearson was a faculty member at the Nikolais/Louis Dance Lab during the time I was a student there. Sara had been a member of Murray Louis' company and now had her own dance company. Classes with Sara were a welcome relief from the strict technical regimen advocated at the Lab. Sara was always willing to give us the time we needed to improvise and explore movements from our own bodies. She worked very hard to shift the responsibility of movement away from an authoritarian teacher back to the student's own impulses where it rightfully belongs.

During our interview, Sara spoke candidly about her eating disorder and its impact on her dancing. We don't have an accurate picture of the number of dancers who struggle with eating disorders though some studies indicate that it is quite common.

Improvisation continues to be key to Sara's artistic process. In some way, it is the gestural equivalent to Gertrude Stein's automatic writing, and it is a useful tool for stepping outside of the boundaries of reason imprinted on the body.

I can't remember a time when I didn't want to dance. I remember waiting till I was five and finally old enough to take my first dance class. Unfortunately, I ended up taking classes at the corner store in the basement with a terrible teacher who wore net stockings and walked around poking her cane into the older girls' legs and stomachs. You learned a routine and performed in a recital once a year. I waited forever to take that class. I don't even know where I got the idea that there was such a thing as class, but my mother must have told me.

At age seven I was old enough to take my first ballet class with a Hungarian man who had danced in the *Ballet Russe de Monte Carlo*. I could hardly wait. Soon I was best in the class, first at the barre. Five years later I was worst in the class, last at the barre. I just wasn't born with the necessary ballet equipment— my feet didn't point, my legs didn't stay up, I had no turnout. Most of class seemed to be spent doing difficult exercises which didn't feel anything like dancing to me. Finally we all turned eleven and it was time to get our first pair of toe shoes. Our feet were individually checked by our teacher, who said I had a strong foot but the arch needed stretching. I passed the inspection, the moment we had all been waiting for had finally arrived, and thus began the humiliating saga which eventually brought an end to my ballet career: I just couldn't get up on my toes, no matter how hard I tried. And because I could only get halfway up, the bottom half of my beautifully darned pink toe shoes became worn and grey while the top half remained bright pink because they never had any contact with the floor. Mortified and filled with shame, I would go out into the street and rub the tops in the gravel, trying to get them to look "right." Ironically, when I joined the Murray Louis Dance Company fifteen years later, the first dance he told me that he planned to choreograph on me was a duet with Rudolf Nureyev— a comedy where I was to wear toe shoes!

I later found out that those ballet classes were quite unusual because we were occasionally asked to improvise. These were my favourite times, the only times when I felt I was really dancing. Mrs. Becker, the pianist, would play four different kinds of music. We were supposed to close our eyes and listen, then dance our interpretation of that music. Invariably, most of the little girls would skip through imaginary fields picking imaginary flowers. I remember once improvising passionately to this dramatic music, playing the roles of two men with one knife, defending their honour and eventually killing each other, surrounded by enormous Roman pillars in a huge marble courtyard. God knows where those images came from, but one thing was certain: I was in my element.

Having given up ballet, I looked around for another outlet. My friends were going to the YWCA, so I joined them and we all took swimming lessons with a woman who shaved her arms (the most memorable part of the experience) and charm classes with a woman who taught us how to cross our legs and how not to cross our legs. It was a boring, surreal time. I also took my first modern dance class which was so bad that I remember everything about it. What impresses me is that through all these years of truly mediocre dance classes, on some intuitive level I knew what dancing was and I knew I had to do it. I knew that I loved it.

That summer I went to Girl Scout camp. One night there was a bonfire program and my favourite older camper who had wild blond hair and wild blue eyes performed a dance around the fire. I was entranced— now *that* was dancing! I got up my courage, went up to her afterwards, and asked, "Is that American Indian dancing? Where can I learn it?" "Oh, no," she said. "That's called improvisation. That's modern dance and I do it with Nancy Hauser." So I got my courage up that fall to make the phone calls to find Nancy Hauser. It took me weeks. I'd go into my mother's bedroom because there was a phone there where I could have privacy. I'd sit, and my hands would get so clammy I couldn't pick up the phone. At first I had to call somebody to find out who this Nancy Hauser was, and get the phone number, and then I called the school. It was, I believe, my first truly independent action. I brought my girlfriend who had gone to ballet class and charm school with me, and we took our first class with Nancy Hauser.

I'll never forget it. Remember, this is St. Paul, Minnesota, 1961. Women are wearing pale pink lipstick and bubble hairdos. This Nancy Hauser woman has pulled-back tight grey hair, with bright, deep red lipstick smeared across her lips. She is wearing a black felt skirt and everybody calls her by her first name, even though she's ten years older than my mother. This wasn't just dance— this was another culture altogether! I just loved it. I just loved it. And I stayed. It was the first place where I found people who shared all the parts of my life.

I knew that I would always dance, but it never occurred to me that it could be a profession, until the summer after I graduated high school. I wouldn't say I-am-a-dancer. Other people in the dance company would say they were dancers when they introduced themselves. I would say, I dance. It wasn't until many years later that I thought I *am* a dancer. This *is* my profession. It happened before I named it.

Throughout my childhood (my failure with ballet left no lasting scars) and even when I started dancing with Nancy I had a very healthy relationship to my body: it looked fine; I was physically healthy and strong; I enjoyed using it; there was no problem at all. And then in about the ninth grade it became fashionable to go on diets. I started to become aware of food in that way but it wasn't a big deal until I started having my first sexual relationship when I was seventeen. It seems as if almost overnight I started to binge. The change was unbelievable. I'd have to diet because I'd binged the night before. This cycle of bingeing and fasting, and this complete obsession with counting calories began. I gained more weight than I ever had, and I stopped going to dance class. I became terribly depressed, couldn't concentrate, and started despising myself and my body for the first time in my life. I remember sitting at my desk, night after night, unable to open a book, crying uncontrollably. What had happened? What was happening? For one thing, I had begun to take birth control pills. Twenty years later, a doctor told me that this extreme personality change and weight gain could have come from the hormonal changes caused by the pills. But was that all? I don't think so. I had been waiting forever to fall in love and have sex with my fantasy poet/singer/philosopher and finally it happened— I was leaving the bourgeois kingdom behind and I was going to be a mysterious, artistic woman!

Instead, sex was a huge disappointment. The relationship was a huge disappointment. And I had no language, no communication skills to deal with him, with it, with myself, with my disappointment, my frustration, my confusion. This pattern repeated itself for many years— when my relationships with lovers, friends, or work were fulfilling (either in fantasy or in a healthier version of reality) my eating obsession became manageable or almost disappeared. When I wasn't getting what I wanted, the "food" spoke louder and louder, getting stronger and stronger. I didn't see this correlation until I was well out of the pattern— when I was submerged in it for over fifteen years, it felt like a story of possession: one moment I was happy, totally absorbed in my life, the next there was only one voice, one thought raging inside of me, getting louder and louder and louder: Eat, eat, eat, eat, EAT!

When I moved to New York at age twenty-four to study with Nik and Murray, the battle lines were clearly drawn: The Enemy was the "Food," which felt to me as if it had unlimited power to imprison and destroy. My weight was the clear representation of who was winning the war. Since our only uniform was leotards and tights, my weakness was fully apparent to the world. An overweight New York dancer introduced me to Overeaters Anonymous, and I followed the program, but there was no spiritual or emotional awakening. I remember enjoying the fellowship and the stories and being confused when a thin woman told of how tired she was of sticking her head in the toilet all night long. I had no idea what she was talking about. One day at the studio, a company member said to me: "Someday we'll have to binge together." I said: "How can you say that? I do everything to avoid it." And she said, "I'll let you in on a secret. I throw up and I'll teach you how." Nobody I knew had ever talked about this before. There was no name for it. I didn't even know this practice existed. Within a few weeks I was throwing up two or three times a day. This went on for five years. I kept it a secret from my husband, who was also in the company. Yes, I managed to get my weight down and generally keep it down. Yes, it gave me some security and control. Yes, it gave me some freedom. And yes, it soon became a living hell. When I wasn't totally absorbed in an activity, the compulsion/obsession/addiction immediately kicked in, and the only way I knew to silence it was to give in and eat— and then throw up. That would give me two hours of freedom before the insanity would begin again. So, for example, I had to arrange my visits with friends to last no more than two hours. I would then make up stories full of deceit and lies so I could sneak off to get my fix. The money I must have spent in those years on my "drug" is unbelievable, the physical damage to my body perhaps irreparable, the emotional devastation it wreaked on my marriage was disastrous. I had no skills to deal with anxiety, anger, frustration, depression, fear, jealousy, boredom. I believed I had a strong spiritual life but it was powerless when it came to the "Food." The addiction never felt as if it had to do with anything but itself. I had no idea or belief that this "weakness" might have to do with my relationship to myself as a woman, with how my culture defines what is acceptable for a woman when it comes to independence and power. I knew how to support, but not how to confront. I would pray to God, begging to be freed of this insanity, saying I would never ask for anything else. I knew I was wasting my life and I was powerless to get out of this addiction. I had tried everything and nothing worked. At this time nobody used the word bulimia. Nobody was talking about eating disorders. Nobody was talking about addiction.

I decided to tell my husband, but I knew if I told him I would have to stop throwing up, and how could I do that without ballooning to four hundred pounds.? By then we had left Murray and Nik and had started our own company. I told him, and his first reaction was hurt— hurt that I had kept this huge part of myself so secret from him for so many years. I returned to Overeaters Anonymous and slowly began to acquire skills to deal with the anxiety, fear, and compulsion. We were touring Europe then. I remember getting through my first breakfast without a binge; then I got through the morning without a binge; and then I got through the morning and lunch without a binge. I added an hour at a time. Then I got through a whole day without a binge and without throwing up. Getting through one day was like a miracle. I had to keep very close guard on my emotional system, and my anxiety level. That was where I first learned to lie down, and I first began taking long, endless baths— those were the first tools I had. To learn to be still instead of running.

Finally, I got through a whole country without throwing up. I got through England, I got through Switzerland, I got through Sweden. And then it was a month, two months, six months. Now it's been over ten years. It wasn't until I rediscovered sex that the inner obsession started to heal. When I got back that sexual energy, Pandora's box exploded! Like many people who came of age in the late sixties with sex and drugs and who later turned to Eastern spirituality, I had believed that celibacy was the goal and that in this world of ideals where God was love, there was no place for negativity, anger, dissatisfaction. When I dropped that early interpretation of spirituality (which left the Indian disciples incredulous at our naïveté and stupidity) and replaced it with a model based on honesty— accepting where I was whether I liked it or not— my relationship to food, sex, and my body began to truly heal and my interest in cultural definitions of male/female woke up for the first time.

Up to this point, all of my choreography was made up of solos and duets, coming out of deep interior landscapes of feeling. My process was private and personal, demanding hours and hours of improvisation. I had no desire and no ideas for group work, nor did I want to work with anyone but my husband. But economics prevailed, and the Laban Centre in London hired us to each choreograph a work on the students. I was terrified. The week before we were to begin, a friend took us to Stonehenge, and I was taken with the energy of Stonehenge and the shape of the rocks. I had this idea of doing a very simple dance about the strength of women. I could never understand why doing a group dance wasn't as satisfying as doing group singing. Group singing was so exhilarating and inspiring, while a group dance was just frustrating. I wanted to make a dance about community and about feeling the power of women. I wanted to make a dance that was as satisfying to do as to watch. I worked with sixteen young women who had never raised their voices! They could raise their legs but not their voices. It was my first non-dance dance, and we all loved it, except for the heads of the Laban Centre. There weren't any fancy steps in it but it was beautiful, and I was happy. I was really happy. I still run into women who had been in the piece and they tell me what an important experience it was for them, how it changed their idea of what dance was, what class could be, what life could be, of how students should be treated. It was all of those things for me as well. I was learning along with them.

For the first thirty-three years of my life, I never thought of dance being about the body. It was through dancing that I transcended the prison of my body. The less I was conscious of my body, the deeper was my connection to dancing. My body hurt. My body had technical limitations. My body was a reminder of the failure of my will, the failure of my belief in God. Dance was my language of motion, energy, dynamics, nuance, direction, timing, texture. Its range was so much bigger and so much smaller than the range allowed in "normal" behaviour. When I danced I had a direct link to the universe inside of me as well as a way of connecting to the universe outside of me. I could think more clearly, feel more deeply, communicate more directly.

In the studio, in the theatre, I felt at home. It didn't matter if it was the dilapidated opera house in Alexandria, Egypt, or the old gym in Dublin, Ireland— I could work, I could play, I could rest. It would be years before I would feel that clear and comfortable in my own apartment.

When I was around thirty-four, I came down with two kinds of hepatitis at the same time. Although the illness lasted only six months, my health, which I had always taken for granted, was shattered, and the past ten years have been a slow recovery process in which, every day, my body teaches, restricts, reminds, encourages, and remembers. The disease knocked out my energy, and I was forced to lie with, to sit with every moment of discomfort, every emotion, every memory without being able to distract myself with any kind of physical activity— no washing the dishes, no reading, no writing, no running across the street to beat the red light. My liver, traditional storehouse for both anger and compassion, had begun to speak and it wouldn't shut up! I began to work with a therapist whose system was based on deep body work meditation, on learning to listen to the body, knowing that one's entire lifetime of experience is literally stored in its rooms and also that one's intuitive wisdom is housed there as well. It was difficult, challenging, delightful work. I remember during the first day we worked together she asked me to sense the outline of my body as I was sitting, talking to her. "Can you feel where you end and the space begins?" she asked. Then I would stand and talk. "Can you feel your feet as you speak? Can you stand a little closer to the floor?" Stand a little closer to the floor? What use of language was that? But I was desperate, and BOOM! Instant change— as if my body were tuned to another level. She encouraged me to stay with discomfort instead of escaping to internal or external oases. To listen to the discomfort and pain. Sometimes it spoke in words, often in movement and rhythms. I began to take this work into my dance classes. I began to radically change what I was teaching and how I was teaching. The way I danced was no longer satisfying. The dances I had made in the past were no longer speaking to me. I was interested in listening more intently to my body and hearing all the stories the different parts of me had to tell. Not only my liver, but my throat, my gut, my tail-bone, my wrists— each had their own rhythms, their own songs, their own secrets. I was fascinated with finding the balance between in and out, with being able to feel me and feel you at the same time. I started talking and dancing at the same time and asking students to do the same. Therapy, dance, history, music, anthropology, all came together. Ideas were coming so quickly it was intoxicating! Teaching, always my clearest strongest place, became the laboratory for these experiments. I changed my warm up to a body work technique founded in my years of Alexander work and the body-based therapy I was practising. I incorporated the Nikolais/Louis philosophy of space, time, motion, and shape into my investigation of emotion and thought, mind and heart. I became fascinated with the psychological aspects of linguistics— the fact that in English, we say ribcage— how does the word cage affect our relationship to that part of our body? Our relationship to breathing? The fact that we say "she works hard" when we mean "she works well." In German, the word for nipple literally translates as breast wart. No doubt that has to say a great deal about the culture's relationship to women. Often, seventy-five percent of my students were foreign born, so we had a wealth of information to draw from in my classes.

My teaching and performing was taking me to England, India,

Korea, Mexico, New Zealand, Greece. I began to see how the cultural roles we inherited as women affected our use of space, our range of dynamics, our choice and lack of choice. In Minnesota the women were supportive and sensitive to each other to such a degree that it was suffocating their artistry. Everything became soft and lyric, no one initiated, no one led, there were no surprises. We talked about it and purposely tried to break those patterns, hopefully expanding their definition of what support can be. In Greece the women loved to argue and loved to confront. Learning to pick up movement from others was their big challenge. They could talk endlessly about art and politics, but ask them to tell a personal story in class as they were moving— forget it! In Korea, the women were trained to be strong, lyric, beautiful, and obedient. Creativity and individuality had been repressed long ago. But how shy, how eager, how hungry they were to change! How ready they were! In Mexico women could be passionate and sexy. Any time men and women danced together it immediately became a stereotyped melodrama of S-E-X. Redefining sensuality, sensation, touch was an incredible experience to witness. Within two weeks a revolution oc-curred. Body tones softened, what people chose to wear to class changed, entire movement vocabularies were transformed. Their bodies began to speak. They began to listen. They were ready, filled with incredible energy and marvelous enthusiasm.

I love seeing people of all sizes and shapes and ages dancing. I think that's one of the most wonderful things that's happened in the past twenty years. When I first moved to New York, that wasn't happening much at all. Of course, for most of the dance world it's no different than it ever was. But in the downtown scene, the world is flipped upside down.

Needless to say, my choreography changed radically. Needless to say, my life changed radically. My marriage didn't survive the change. At age thirty-six I was beginning again, confronting my dependency on men, on teachers, on energy. My classes reflected those changes— I became committed to helping dancers learn how to work alone, how to work on their own. Dance is a social art form. You go to a special place to do it, you always do it with other people under the direction and support of a teacher. When people— especially women— try to begin to work independently in a studio, they often have tremendous difficulty. So I began to teach everything with that in mind— to help people find their own enthusiasm, their own motivation. Practising dancing with nobody watching, practising with everybody watching. To learn to make decisions. To learn to listen. To speak. To direct. To follow. To connect. To separate. To begin. As they learned, I learned. And learning to take what I was learning in the studio into life outside the studio. To listen to and respect my body's needs at home, on the street, in the office. The body doesn't lie. The body remembers. The body reveals. It's difficult work. I'm still a beginner.

Dance is my teacher, dance is my friend, dance is my therapist, and dance is my playground. It's available to me wherever I am, all of the time— or sometimes none of the time. I'm still a beginner.

SUSANA
GALILEA

I have known Susana Galilea since we both arrived as new students at the Nikolais/Louis Dance Lab during the fall semester of 1984. From her arrival, Susana attracted a lot of attention from teachers and colleagues. Susana is an exceptionally gifted dancer with a very strong sense of rhythm and movement. Her body intuits movement. The school directors were impressed with her work, but they could not accept her body. It is too large.

Susana's body does not fit the conventional image of the slender dancer. For that reason, she has had to make her own way in the dance world. Changing audience expectations of what a dancer should look like has become a crusade of sorts for Susana, but it does not dominate her choreography. Because of her size, her presence on stage challenges audiences to see and feel qualities of dance beyond those presented by the image of the dancer's body. After watching Susana perform, an audience can no longer equate a thin body with a good dancer and a fat body with a bad dancer.

I don't know if I decided to study ballet or if my mother decided to send me to class, but as far as I remember I was interested in dance. I did a couple of years of ballet and at the same time I did gymnastics with parallel bars so I was quite active. During the second year of ballet they put me into toe shoes. I remember going through the blisters and the blood. I loved the feeling. Of course, everybody wanted to be a ballerina.

It was very painful, but it was not something you questioned. You just dreamed about it. From the beginning, I was always the fattest one in class. My body is not made for the rigorous technique of the turnout or maybe I was never interested enough to pursue it to be technically proficient but I was always very musical, very lyrical. I could do whatever

I was told and there was an involvement in movement that was always there. I enjoyed it. Of course, I was always told to suck my stomach in and get rid of my butt which I could never do.

It's hard for me to remember how I used to feel as opposed to how I feel now. I'm sure that I saw the other bodies and was very envious and wished I could be that way but that didn't stop me from dancing either. And then I stopped. I stopped and it was a big blur until I turned sixteen. Then my mother took me to a gymnastic class, but it was different because it was oriented to losing weight.

My body was always cause for concern, at least as far as my family was concerned. It was always something to do something about. I have a feeling that I got into dance to survive because it was the only way my family would leave me alone. And I was actually good; people noticed me. With dance, I was doing something with my body other than being looked at and told that I have to get rid of all this extra weight.

I've never thought that I couldn't dance because of my body. My body made me self-conscious and I was very often under attack or discriminated against. The fears I had were the same fears I had on the street. I just happened to be in a unitard which made things all that much worse. I don't think I ever doubted that I could dance because obviously I could dance and nobody was going to tell me that I couldn't.

Up to today dance is one of the only places where I feel comfortable, especially in performance. I may be concerned about what I look like up to two seconds before stepping on stage. Once I'm on stage I couldn't care less. In class, if you're uncomfortable with your body, you keep it with you like you do the rest of the day. It has depended a lot on the teacher and the approach or the focus of the class. It's hard for me to remember objectively what my experience has been up to now. I know my size has always been a factor in one way or another. It has always been double-sided because people have said they would take me into their company if I were skinnier, but what kind of message is that? It pushed me into taking a different road and I'm happy doing my work and finding people who appreciate me no matter what. Yet it does take a lot of choices out of my hands. There are some people I may want to work with and there is no chance I will. Sometimes I go to auditions and they don't even look at me. But I don't think it's any different than people who are too short or too tall or who don't fit into the costume they are looking to replace.

At the same time, people notice me. Because of my body they don't expect me to be able to dance, yet if I were thinner, they would just assume I'm a good dancer. I stand out.

I felt a little like a pariah, outside of the dance cliques in Spain. The last year I was in the north of Spain they invited me to be a teacher and a choreographer. That year was very positive. Then I came to New York and I went through so much here. Dance is the world I move in now.

I was so excited. I couldn't wait. I had been planning this move for years. I always knew I wanted to come to New York. I had subscribed to *Dance Magazine* and seen all the things that were going on. I had no idea of the extent of this change because I had been such a loner all my life. I had travelled so much in Europe and been alone so much and done so many things alone that I thought this is just the same thing. I had a romantic dream of seeing Broadway, shows and pictures. Everything looked very glamorous. It was a big adventure.

It may have been more difficult for me here because of the beauty standards in America. Where I come from it's very different. Morphologically, people are made differently. We are more African. There is a very different approach to beauty. There is a dark kind of beauty. When you get here you are supposed to look like Hollywood. I felt very inappropriate and inferior because these people looked exactly like the dance magazine pictures I had been seeing and I didn't. Also, in Spain I had been the teacher. Everybody worshipped me. I was in a remote part of Spain where they hadn't seen much dance and I was bringing jazz and modern dance to them. It was humiliating. It all went together with relocating to this culture.

The body image here is very violent. The standard of beauty here is very violent, the way people treat themselves. Everything is tight. You have to be tight, better not breathe in any sense and if you have IT, you have IT and if you don't, you don't. Then it becomes a matter of natural selection really and there is nothing I can do. Maybe if I starve myself to death and spend my life in the gymnasium I would be like that. But I just don't have the time and it's never been such a priority that I've been willing to do that. It never occurred to me. I always say I am just not made this way. I'll never know because I will never have the motivation to do that, so I'm working on the other end of it which is accepting my body as it is and using it as it is.

I imagine a lot of people come into dance to worship themselves in the mirror and that is fostered by many educators and choreographers. I never had that solace so I really had to concentrate on other things. If I just stood there looking in the mirror I didn't like what I saw so I had better move because there is nothing else in it for me. I work without a mirror for a purpose. I can't stand looking into a mirror. When I look into the mirror I see what people see and somehow I've never felt that I am as big as I am. When I look into the mirror I see how big I am and then I say, "Oh, my goodness," but when I don't look into the mirror I don't have the sense that I look like that. Maybe it's because it doesn't matter. To me dance has never been the body. It's been the movement. I feel with the movement and it really has never been the body.

In front of the whole class Murray Louis told me and another dancer who was fleshy and round that we had to get rid of all our extra fat; otherwise we were always going to be slaves to our bodies and our image. The only way to get past that and really focus on the movement and dance was not to have to bother about issues of weight. At the time, I was very impressionable but now that I think about it, it's completely the other way around. These people are not questioning the status quo in the world of dance. All of these choreographers who have come to me and said, "You can be in my company if only... " and "You'll never make it unless you lose the weight," are catering to what people want to see. People are used to seeing these bodies and that's what they're going to give. They don't want to take the chance to put me on stage.

Somebody is going to complain. But why don't they take the chance? They are not taking risks. They are not willing to question anything or to risk anything. Why do people have to look that way? Who says? It's just the way it's been. To me right now it's very important to upset that perception and I'm getting a kick out it. It's your loss. I started really thinking that it is their loss after a while and I don't concern myself with it so much. Okay, so I'm not going to be in a company. It's been a very powerful issue because you see how people react to it.

The turning point for me was the Haitian dance classes because suddenly I was a goddess. There was nothing I needed to do with my body in order to dance now, and immediately people began to appreciate me. In that world nobody ever said anything to me other than, "Oh my God, I wish I had your curves because it looks so good." You see the kind of people who go to Haitian class— all kinds of shapes, all kinds of ages, all kinds of everything. Suddenly I found a dance form that was all inclusive. Suddenly it was very healing. Suddenly it was a movement that made more sense to me. Somehow it came more easily to me whereas the other didn't.

Ethnic dance always has a higher purpose. It is celebratory. It's for a god. It's for something else. It's not to look good for yourself or for your teacher. It's such a different kind of focus. And I started really feeling very different because I was totally accepted. Not only was I accepted; I was lusted after completely! It was very nice to be lusted after, but that was not the point. I just happened to fit a certain aesthetic.

A month after starting Haitian dance classes I was performing in a Haitian dance performance. Haitian dance made complete sense to my body. Culturally, it saved my life. For a very long time nothing made sense to me culturally in this city. I still struggle with that. Then I started Shiatsu and Haitian dance. Both of these ways of working with the body are from different cultures— Asian and Caribbean. They're both about something else than your ego. That saved my life and then I could stand being here.

When you're doing Haitian dance, you have no time to look in the mirror and I had already been doing that all my life. I'd better not look in the mirror because it's too depressing. You see something different when you look at yourself in motion as opposed to being still. If you're looking into the mirror, something is wrong because then there is a part of you that is not into the movement. I've never been a mirror person. I rehearse without a mirror. I can't rehearse with a mirror because then I just look.

I believe more in video because then you are moving. But it's rough for me to look at the video, because all I see is my big butt, although my attitude is starting to change. I don't care as much about the big butt.

I still have a problem with what my body says about me. I'm scared that the body says a lot of things I don't want it to say or that people are going to interpret my size. Like, I'm not professional enough because if I were professional I would be skinny or if I danced enough I would lose the weight. People have their own preconceptions about what bodies mean.

Not many people of my size have made it where I have because many of them got discouraged on the way or got discouraged even before starting. I think I have a responsibility to tell the world that it is possible and there are other people doing it but it is a very small minority of people. When you are fat, people want you to do dances that talk about the body. To me that's another challenge. You want me to deal with something you don't want to deal with. You want me to do your work for you, to deal with the fact that I am a fat person dancing. It's like if you're Asian, you have to do something Asian. That's just discrimination. Right now I want to be on stage and do a completely abstract piece because I don't have to talk about the fact that I am whatever I am. I want to do what I do.

This body racism is completely rampant in dance. It is one of the building blocks in dance and everybody suffers from it. There are perfectly thin people who are being told horrible things who become anorexic. Or people who are short who are not given opportunities or people who are too tall or who have too large breasts. Especially if you're a woman. If you're a guy they'll take you because there are so few of them but if you're a woman there isn't such a big market. There are so many horses. You can take whatever you want and be picky. To me it's like one of the big conspiracies. It is a conspiracy in the world at large but in the world of dance there is such secrecy around it. Everybody takes it for granted. Everybody puts up with it because everybody wants the opportunity to be taken into a company and appreciated. Nobody talks about it. Nobody questions it. Nobody stands up for themselves, including myself at times.

It's a given that if you're in dance you have to take care of your body. You have to be thin. You just don't question that. If you're a painter you have to work at it and if you're a musician you have to practise and if you're a dancer you have to practise. Nobody tells you what kind of practice. They tell you you have to have technique and you should go to ballet class so you can do whatever you want afterward.

The other day, I taped two dances by Balanchine and I looked at them and thought, "This is boring." There is nothing here, just nice conventional steps and conventional bodies. They all look the same. If Balanchine was completely self-contained with a group of masochistic women working together, and everybody acknowledged that, then I could look at it and accept what they've created as amazing because it's a crazy thing that doesn't touch me at all. But it's considered the norm against which you are measuring yourself. And to me it's a lunacy. If somebody wants to do it, fine! I'm not going to stop them, but don't touch me! The worse thing that's ever happened is this mystification around dancers, about them not having a life, not marrying because then you have babies and you have to quit your career. Or even the thought that not everybody can dance, that only privileged people can dance. It's only for a certain kind of person with a certain kind of craziness in them. You have to be dedicated and sacrifice yourself. All this talk about sacrifice, sacrifice, sacrifice— I think that's the worst thing that's ever happened to ballet and to dance. That's why I'm interested in humanity in dance because I want to see people on stage, people with experience and with a life who dance. I don't want to see somebody who has been put in a little bubble by a crazy old man from the age of twelve on. If that's what I am seeing, I want to know that's what I am seeing and I want to know that it's a certain kind of craziness called the Balanchine Company. I don't want to think this is the highest art that ever existed. I don't want to hear dance talked about only in that way.

I'm a great believer in longevity. Even with injuries, they are just things you have to adjust to. I don't see myself doing anything else. Sometimes I think, my God, if I lose my legs... Yet there are people in wheelchairs dancing. Dance is where I feel the most me. It's my creativity. It's what I do. It's what has been given to me. I really feel it's a gift.

JOHANNA
BOYCE

As we were finishing the interview I asked Johanna if she wanted to add anything more. "Yes," she said, "My seven-year-old daughter is extremely preoccupied with her weight and it's very discouraging to me. What I see on TV and in the culture is this incredible focus on thinness and firmness. This fixation didn't used to hit until adolescence. Now it's in primary school. And it really saddens me. Little girls barely have a chance to just experience themselves unless you isolate them from the culture." In a piece choreographed before moving to Vermont with her family, Johanna addressed this issue. How do we, as women, grow up feeling about our bodies and how does our culture shape these feelings? I was part of this piece and was impressed with Johanna's ability to create a supportive environment for exploring tender issues and with her ability to transform this raw material into a performance. Surrender, Mouth to Breast, explicitly deals with many of the issues Johanna has explored throughout her dance career: building a community of women, the weight and raw energy of the female body. Since this piece, Johanna has not danced or choreographed; a second child and middle-age have changed her focus. She characterizes this phase as a natural fallow period, a promise no doubt of more insightful work.

When I was in college I auditioned with everyone else who wanted to get into dance classes. It wasn't set up as an audition, per se. It was a class to place people according to their dance abilities. But I was placed out of a lot of classes, and the only explanation I could really determine for myself was my size. The ballet teacher talked to me about my weight, and said there were some things she felt I couldn't do. I had more weight than she thought the particular ballet technique warranted. So I created classes for myself, and other people who didn't get into those classes. We did workshops in the afternoon to explore movement ideas. I think that was a first kind of rebellion or separation. I wasn't terribly interested in what the ballet classes were offering, but I was hurt that I hadn't been included. And I think from that sadness and anger I decided to rebel, or to distinguish myself and make something of greater interest to compete with that other notion of dance.

I had taken dance classes when I was little, and when I was in prep school. Also my mother had a propensity towards dance. She was a good dancer and she loved ballroom dancing. There was an identification with her and her encouragement around taking dance classes but it wasn't really until I was in college that I seized on dance as a means for personal expression. At the same time, my brother had been paralyzed in a swimming accident. The paralysis issue sent my family into a frenzy and didn't leave me as much room to express what was going on for me. And so, I think I found this creative outlet to speak through.

I was sixteen when my brother had his accident and eighteen when he died. The aftermath of this loss took place when I was eigtheen to twenty-two. He was the closer of my two brothers to me, and he was twenty-four. Dancing gave me the means to emotionally express myself and to be able to say things that were too complicated to put into words. That's why it reverberated for me so much, and was part of why it became so important to me at that age.

One of the first autobiographical pieces I did, that started giving me a name for that kind of work, was a piece in which I talked about his accident and death. And also another loss which happened at about the same time during my first real relationship with a man. This person was from El Salvador, and I lost him through the revolution. So the two stories intertwine. They are about a young girl coming of age, and coming to see the world outside of herself with all of its struggles, both personal and political. That piece helped me enunciate the enormity of the pain and it helped me have an expression for the hurt and the cruelty that happens in the world. And also, perhaps, the connection of excess weight to pain. I was very unabashed about my weight, flinging myself around in non-dance ways and using the body as a buffer, rather than a piece of beauty or a sculpture that should be seen or treated in a certain way.

I went to Middlebury College, a liberal arts school in Vermont. At the time the College had a very sophisticated art and theatre program with a lot of connections to the current art scene in New York City. So I had a lot of interaction with teachers in New York, and with students who were involved in conceptual art and dance. I was hearing a lot about that, and trying those ideas on. It was a very intellectually informed venture with a lot of seeding from other fields. In the workshops I took a lot of ideas from other fields. I would take pictures or art ideas that we were learning in design and tell people to move according to cards that had slashes, dots, and splotches on them.

My understanding of modern dance was generative. Martha Graham studied with Loïe Fuller, Paul Taylor studied with Martha Graham, Merce Cunningham studied with her, and then the next generation studied with them. It was generative and you broke off from it and defined yourself. When I came along it was allowed to take from anywhere and start from anywhere: pick from this, take from that, reject this. It was more of an eclectic form, so that almost anything could happen. It was all open, up for grabs. The whole pedestrian movement with Yvonne Rainer, Patricia Brown, and Lucinda Childs was at its height. They were all doing pieces that had nothing to do with dance. I knew about that, and from knowing that, had permission to say, "Yes, heavy people can dance."

In the culture of Western modern dance, there are certain movement patterns that are symbolic and are understood as signs that suggest dance: a certain heightened awareness of grace and ease, shape and form, that accents beauty and muscularity. People, as cultures do, have a certain generalized concept of what that all means. I felt the restrictions of that, and the limitations of an arabesque, for example, or a Humphrey fall and recovery. A lot of it makes movement sense in terms of effortlessness, or a productivity of grace, but it is limited in its scope and in what it can communicate. It suggested a kind of cultural hauteur or finesse that infuriated me, the assumption that there is only one acceptable way to communicate those ideas.

I always felt dance was a female province. It was one area in which women could reign supreme, predominantly because it allowed emotional expression. (Although seeing women only as emotionally expressive is a bit frightening to me.) When ideas started coming in, there was more of a male contribution. Steve Paxton was very influential to me, because he once said that every movement is part of his dance vocabulary— picking up a chair, getting out of bed in the morning. All those people kept opening up and validating my experience of that, too. I felt that the other arts were more male-dominated than dance. Also there were many women dancing and many women watching; there were a lot of men watching, too, which I think kept some of the focus on beauty and eroticism in dance.

I graduated from Middlebury and worked for a while as an international student advisor in a small college in New Hampshire where I also taught dance. I was dissatisfied with that and ended up moving to New York. Within six months of moving to New York I had produced my own concert and was invited to perform at The Kitchen. The new things I put together once I got to New York must have grown out of the incubation in college. When I went to New York I saw so much that I thought was repetitive and redundant coming from people my age. I felt as if they were reinventing the wheel. And I thought, I can do something as interesting as this, and went right ahead.

At the time you could do performances in your own loft, so it felt personal and workshop-related. When I first was doing the work, we rehearsed it in the space we performed it in. It was my living room, and I didn't do much but walk around the neighbourhood and put up posters. It had that familiarity to it, so I didn't feel like I was crossing into another culture. There were times later when I was performing in different places and felt the clash more between the workshop and the performance space.

When I first started in New York I was doing more group pieces with a male-female group. Part of my skill is working with people and bringing out their strengths, organizing groups to convey a community effect that is yearned for. That has a strong feeling for the audience, in witnessing the way my people work together. A lot of my pieces offer hope; they're often yearnings or longings, or wishes for humans to be heard or seen in certain ways. Or as a community of people working together.

In a piece called *The Pass*, I had four women and four men passing through different interactions with each other, and passing objects amongst themselves. They had layered T-shirts they took off as they moved from activity to activity. Eventually they completely disrobed and passed each other down. At the end, they drank from cups passed to each other before they left the stage. It was choreographed chaos. There was a sense that things were happening organically, and moving unpredictably from one thing to another. But suddenly there would be a whole, a completely different structure happening with its own inherent order. And I think it was different from some of the pieces where people had used pedestrian movements before, because there was this underlying organizational structure that you couldn't quite see moment to moment, but found yourself noticing from time to time. It distinguished itself from the "happenings" of the sixties and the seventies where there was a lot of group activity that was either improvisational, or wasn't organized for a specific effect, and yet it still had a naturalistic quality. That piece catapulted me into post-modern awareness and stardom as far as that happens in that genre. It was very well-received critically. The acclaim made me feel I could do this work, and what I was interested in was of value to other people. These were people who were not dancers, and it was an acknowledgment to me that there were people hungry to be freed from the restrictions.

I was still using the work as a way to say something I could not quite believe myself, which was you didn't have to fit the cultural norm to be accepted. It was gratifying to have external acceptance of that, but it didn't release me from my own anxieties about it. I found the freedom that I have from it through my own personal work, not from being in the performing arts or in the dance world.

I have two styles. One is working with large groups, creating patterns or kaleidoscopic effect with or without content, separate from movement. And the other is solo, direct personal expression or interactive expression, where the work is more intimate and autobiographical, life's history expressed. I also work with a combination of those styles— a group kaleidoscopic effect with personal history. This happened with the last piece I worked on, *Surrender, Mouth to Breast*. It was the first time I had done individual history with more than two people at a time.

I like working with objects, particularly when I work with people who are not performers, because the objects give them a focus on the activity they are doing. And it is a genuine focus, rather than an artificial presentation to the audience. So the audience is witnessing someone going through something somewhat dangerous, or an activity that has a beginning and an end.

In a piece called *Incidents in Coming of Age*, which was also autobiographical, I had two women and one man join me. It was an exploration of my family's relation to my brother's experience as a Seal in Vietnam, and my experience as a thirteen-year-old girl with a very aggressive and violent older brother. While I was trying to find my identity he was participating in enormous violence which was being held up as a standard. I got a lot of acclaim for that piece because it asked questions about gender identity. I think the piece helped my elder brother become aware that I existed at all in the world, that I might have had experience separate from his. The piece was done during the time people were just beginning to talk about Vietnam again, so it brought back to him a lot of the things he had tried to bury. I have to assume some of my pieces have been quite painful for my family, but they enjoy the acclaim my pieces bring and the excitement of getting good reviews.

It's always been difficult for me as a choreographer to be in a piece. When you want to express something either physically, emotionally, or intellectually you have to be in that space to get to it. But then you have to stand outside of the piece and look at it to see whether or not you're communicating. When I did my group pieces, it was much easier for me to conduct from the outside to determine if what I wanted to see was coming across. When I did the solo pieces it was almost improvisational. The piece depended a lot on the moment and how I used the space in which I was performing. The focus was less on the exterior, on the way it looked. I believed that if the expression was genuine and of the moment, the piece would work.

I've been influenced by the women's movement. How can any thinking woman not be? For me it has been more about celebrating women's diversity, beauty, and power rather than fighting against something. And my work has been about revelling in, and pointing out, for our enjoyment, all the different ways women can be highlighted and appreciated. I've been part of that whole flood and have always wanted to get the message out very strongly.

After I gave birth to my daughter Charlotte, I created a piece that focused on water and women. The experience of water breaking inside me, the swelling of one's self, the milk flowing from my body, the generation of life inspired that piece. That piece steered me toward a kind of femininity I had shied away from, or was a little afraid to embrace because the balance is so often held in that favour. But in this piece I accepted this part of womanness and wanted to focus on the more mystical and magical part of life, the life-forces flowing from women. It was a very slow piece, calm and soothing, embracing some of the virtues of motherhood.

At one point I had really liked the success of previous pieces with women talking to women, women moving with women and I wanted a format that continued that. I was also interested in the experience of women in community. At the same time, I decided the critical acclaim I had was about a split personality. People either adored the autobiographical work I was doing, or they adored the community group work. I couldn't find anyone who seemed to like both of them. I was beginning to become dissatisfied with critical acclaim in general, and I wasn't as interested in touring the pieces any more. It was more important to me to create them, to see them realized and move on, rather than repeating them to keep myself alive by touring. I started looking for other ways of making money. At that time I was beginning to study psychotherapy, and I think that my study, combined with the interest in making a community of women, made me focus on the idea of a workshop growing into a performance.

I also felt that although many of my pieces dealt indirectly with weight, I had never tackled it straight on, and surprisingly I had never seen anyone else really talk about the body and the experience of being on stage in a dance in a body, not only using yourself as art but when your art doesn't fit the mode. Those three things combined to create the structure for *Surrender, Mouth to Breast* in which women came together for ten weeks or so to talk about their experiences of being female in the culture and to talk specifically about their bodies. Could we present both our vulnerability and our strength in one piece and how could we support each other in doing that? Since that piece, I haven't been quite as interested in the narcissistic attention I get from performing. Initially that aspect of it was a propelling factor for me. But now I feel more like really studying whatever the issue is. I feel like I'm in a gestative time for a bigger idea.

A lot of dance people see is youth-oriented. If we go dancing or do dancing, it's very energetic. It's an excitable art form, not a passive art form. And I think the emphasis in our culture on aerobics and sports, has really taken that kind of energetics to a new height. Sometimes I think I'd like to wait another ten or twenty years before I make my next statement. I'd like to be much older because I think something needs to be expressed for that generation. Some people have older people dance with them, but often they still have them doing dance things. Why do they have to do arabesques? Or move in a dancer-like fashion? I notice as I'm getting older, that I'm definitely slowing down. Things take more effort to do, and I'm not as interested in doing them. I assume I am not alone and I want to have a way to keep saying things in this genre without having to adapt to a certain level of grace or energy.

CROWSFEET
DANCE
COLLECTIVE

Crowsfeet Dance Collective was one of the two groups formed from the Wallflower Order Dance Collective, which was a women's dance group founded in Eugene, Oregon, in 1975. Committed to increasing political awareness and social action through their art, the Wallflower Order explored various techniques and toured extensively in the United States, Canada, Europe, and Latin America. When the collective went through major changes in 1984, Suchi Branfman, Pamela Gray, Andrea Ko Harmin, Marel Malaret, and Dana Sapiro decided to stay together to continue this work. They formed the Crowsfeet Dance Collective, a multicultural group of dancers with a base in the San Francisco Bay area and an office in New York City.

Suchi Branfman grew up in California where she studied ballet as a child. Later she studied modern dance and moved to New York City, studying with Viola Farber and Gus Solomon, Jr., among others. She taught in several schools and universities on the East Coast and performed with different companies before joining the Wallflower Order.

Marel Malaret grew up in San Juan, Puerto Rico, where she studied ballet, flamenco, and jazz dance. In 1976 she moved to New York City where she studied at Barnard College and graduated in dance from New York University in 1982, having concentrated on modern, jazz, and the Dunham technique. She has taught at different studios in New York City and worked with community programs in East Harlem. She joined the Wallflower Order in 1983.

SUCHI BRANFMAN: In the Crowsfeet Dance Collective (CDC) we learn and purposefully choose to work from a multicultural base and our material reflects this international perspective. The way I see it, this is a natural progression for the Wallflower Order Dance Collective (WODC) because as we started developing politically and working with other people we opened up our vision to a bigger picture of society. We started dealing with class, racism, apartheid, liberation struggles, and the effect of our government on these issues. We expanded our vision and continue to bring our perspective both as women and from our varied backgrounds to these issues in a personal way, so hopefully our work is not didactic but personal as well.

MAREL MALARET: Mostly the divisions started as WODC began integrating and developed from a white middle class women's group to the understanding that this society is composed of many cultures and races. Also as WODC developed politically and people joined political parties we had to deal with the fact that not everybody supports the same political lines. How do you go on working as a collective, integrate the group, and deal with political differences? People became frustrated and basically it exploded, so we stopped working together and reached a compromise. When I look back and try to explain it I don't think the differences could have been solved. They were irreconcilable. We were not trying to pull back together and settle our differences. We were going two different ways. The problem was how do we make the decision.

SUCHI: Everyone in CDC has trained in different areas.

MAREL: But we all have trained in some way as dancers, so we all, talking about it, have a common standard.

SUCHI: We could say that we all have a common base, in that we have all studied ballet. We have come to realize that generally people in this country believe that if you have trained in ballet or a rigorous modern technique then you have "good technique." African, Afro-

Haitian, Afro-Caribbean, or Cuban dance are never included in what is called "high quality" technical training. It is a very Westernized and racist standard of technique and we are trying to break with that.

In workshops we talk about what the standard is and why. In fact it is very racist and ethnocentric because there are other levels of strength, power, and technique in those other movements. I have learned a lot from...

MAREL: ... the diversity. For example we have a highly trained dancer who was a principal with the Joffrey Ballet and the Alvin Ailey Dance Theatre. Because of our different training we move differently, which is very exciting on stage, so we are able to have these different kinds of dancing, choreography, and approaches in our show.

SUCHI: And then we are all training in other things at different times. In our workshops, which change as we learn and evolve, we teach many different things. In a workshop we don't expect people to become experts in anything. They probably won't make an incredible piece but they will get a flavour for many things. It will give them possibilities, new ways to look at and deal with the creative process, and also other things to think about while they are doing their work.

MAREL: The main goal of our workshops, and of our work, is how to use different tools to give out a message. We use sign language, martial arts, theatre, and song, so when we teach choreography we try to have people experience these different tools and combine them with dance movement. All kinds of people come to our workshops, although the participants are still mainly women from the women's movement. We would like to do more outreach.

SUCHI: And we still can't afford to give enough scholarships for those who can't afford to pay. We still don't provide child care and people who work can't easily come to a three week workshop from ten a.m. to nine p.m. There are many contradictions because we can't afford to do certain things even though we would like to.

MAREL: We have political study groups. We bring in women to talk, short films, materials to read. We stress that people are dancers, but not just dancers. They are interested in doing cultural work and in growing, using art for their political work. It is not limited to dancers. People who are not dancers can be very creative.

SUCHI: For most of the workshop we put people together, but we do technique classes in levels which some people find hard to deal with. There is the concept that dividing people according to levels is incorrect.

MAREL: It's right in a practical way; you don't want people getting injured...

SUCHI: Also people learn different things at different times. It doesn't mean that those who are more advanced are better people or even necessarily better dancers. It's just where they are in terms of their training.

MAREL: It has a lot to do with who we are also. As dancers we don't have to go up on stage and just be technically good. We have to project, be politically committed, act, choreograph. I have a lot of respect for a beginner class because I know I can take it and work in a variety of ways. But this society teaches us that words like beginner and advanced have negative connotations.

SUCHI: In our workshops technique is not over-emphasized. We also teach choreography in which very often the most creative and least limited stuff comes from people who haven't had as much training, but are doing what is coming from themselves. We purposefully don't divide that into levels. We say the goal of this is not to make a dance but is a chance to see what all your options are. We also spend a lot of time talking. People get to know each other and open up issues in study groups such as: Who becomes a dancer? Why? Who doesn't? How do you take class? And then we address the larger issues of how to integrate work into society and make it accessible.

MAREL: Basically our political goal is to make dance accessible to people. We try in our show and with the group to be artists who are a part of society. This doesn't mean all of our dances are political in the way we usually think of the word. We also educate people with the music we choose, with the way we dance.

SUCHI: This touches on the fact that dance performances, in addition to being educational and politicizing, are also entertainment. This issue often comes up for people who want to do political art work or political performance because all of a sudden the evil word entertaining appears. But entertainment is what gets in there and does something to people's spirit.

MAREL: That's what art does.

SUCHI: And then you put something on top of it and it becomes powerful, wonderful, and inspiring. Don't say it can't be entertaining because it is. It makes you think. It makes you respond. It can and should do all of these things.

MAREL: It's very political.

SUCHI: Yes, it's so easy to think political means a certain thing and it doesn't. That doesn't mean we don't have priorities. We do. We spend a lot of time talking about what we want to say and why. What is the best tool? Are we succeeding? What is our audience response? Then we say we want a dance-like piece, we want to wear bright colours.

MAREL: It's the endless dialogue of artists doing political work. I was discussing this with Luis Enrique Julia (Puerto Rican classical guitarist) who is a member of Conjunto Cespedes, a group which plays Cuban folklore. Their songs do not talk about revolution and they get a lot of criticism because of that, yet they are from Cuba and support Cuba. They want to establish ties between this society and Cuba and they do it through entertainment. Many people who would never go to a political rally or to a CDC performance do go and dance to the music of Conjunto Cespedes. The music they play is a political act in itself and that's what he considers an important part of his political work to be.

SUCHI: Chris Iijma wrote an article that we've discussed intensely in workshops in which he says that form, content, and context are all political ways of dealing with issues. People very often think of the content as political, but the context can also be political. For example, after the Cuban revolution the Cuban Ballet Company performed in the cane fields. Maybe the content wasn't political, but the context was in terms of taking ballet to workers who had never seen ballet before.

MAREL: And then there is the other evil word, "commercial." When good, conscious artists become commercially viable, everybody criticizes them; but that artist, depending on his or her consciousness, will have the means to reach a broader audience. Given the chance to do an MTV video I would run for it, put punk clothes on, and say something, because that is what is reaching everybody and how a whole society is being indoctrinated. It is a way of reaching an audience because touring and producing is certainly more limited in North America compared to Mexico, for example, where we performed at a festival where the show was free.

SUCHI: That is a big dilemma for us, because if you want to work professionally you want to get paid, which means you have to go to a community that will pay you, which means there has to be someone in the community who considers it important to bring in cultural groups. If there is not, we can make the choice (which we frequently do) to train a producer and say we will work with you very closely and will just take a portion of the door. But we can only do a limited amount of that.

MAREL: You need a society that is more conscious of bringing culture to its people. You need organizations that can afford to produce festivals and make it very open for the whole population to be interested in culture. We do so much work trying to get the company on its way that for us to say we are going to perform for free, while we are waitressing and trying to make a living, is not possible.

SUCHI: Block booking is one way to do it. Also performing in community spaces and trying different ways of getting funding. Libraries have programming money even if it is minimal, community centres also have money. Trying to resource into your community also broadens the audience and the people who go to the performance by putting it into a space people go to. It's making the choice of going to the community rather than going to dance spaces that only dance audiences go to.

Breaking the alienation starts way before the performance, in the choice of a producer who will do outreach in the community. In the performance situation itself we usually warm up on stage and encourage people to come in before the show. We play music while people are coming in and at the end we applaud the audience because they have given us the material, the impetus, and the inspiration to do our work. We also introduce ourselves at the beginning of the performance. Usually we dedicate the show to someone or talk about what is going on in the world or whatever action is happening in that town. We do this on purpose so we can break down that barrier and the audience can see us talking. We are people, you are people and now we are going to perform and hope you like it. We thank people and we encourage them to talk to us.

MAREL: And we take it very seriously. We encourage them to give feedback and people do come to talk to us. A lot of pieces have changed gradually because of the feedback we get.

SUCHI: We could do more. We would love to stay the following day and have a workshop about how we work, find out how you work, teach some movement, but we often can't afford to, because if we perform Friday night in Chicago, we can perform Saturday night in Milwaukee. Economically, producers can rarely afford to pay us to stay two days.

The feedback we have gotten from performing in places like Nicaragua and Mexico and also the influence that has had on our work are to me the most hopeful and positive responses. I see myself as part of a much larger thing and can see so clearly that our work is not alien to people but is something that inspires them and makes them think.

I've also learned a lot from working with Grupo Raiz, with Marel, Pam, all the different people we work with, learning what their reality is, seeing how it comes out on stage and in our internal process.

MAREL: We have been in situations that haven't seemed positive at first but have had positive outcomes. For example, when we were touring with Grupo Raiz, we found ourselves in places where women's production companies did not want to produce us because we were performing with men. When we discussed it with the producers we found that they themselves were divided. A majority had voted to produce only Wallflower Order but it had created dialogue among them about producing women artists who also work with men.

SUCHI: Or when someone said to us, "You used to dance about women and you just don't any more." Yet when we looked at the show in that light we found that there *were* pieces about women but they weren't all about women she knows. The pieces were about black women, women in Nicaragua, women in El Salvador, women in South Africa.

MAREL: For us, all our pieces are about women. They all come from our perspective as women and they all deal with women.

SUCHI: Another discussion we have had with other women performers in women's festivals concerns the idea that whatever we create is okay because it is created by women. As a group our response is, "Fine, but as women we have to take responsibility for what we say and do, for how we do it and who we do it with."

MAREL: We are part of a society made of not only women. We have also heard the criticism that WODC is not feminist, it's leftist. Does one exclude the other? Obviously for us, one isn't exclusive of the other, but for some people or producers it is.

SUCHI: The other discussion we have had concerns sexual preference. Before class, racial, or cultural backgrounds are brought up, people will ask about the sexual preference of the members in our group. We address that question by turning it around and stating what we do have. We address women's issues from so many levels that we refuse to identify ourselves as a lesbian collective. We prefer to look at ourselves from another point of view— which is a difference from WODC. There was a time when WODC was separatist and woman identified. CDC is woman identified, but that doesn't exclude being internationally and cross-culturally identified.

The despairing aspect of it has so much to do with economics because we are not getting any younger. It sounds funny but it is a concern as we get older, as we have mothers in the group, as other people want to have children, as we want to be able not to have to work every minute.

For years now we have been working constantly to keep the group alive and sometimes we haven't been able to pay ourselves. Whenever we have, the pay has been minimal and there are no benefits.

MAREL: Just trying to make a living and survive and do the amount of work it takes to make the company go is impossible. We work in our spare time. Dance classes are expensive. How do you keep yourself in shape? And when do you take classes?

SUCHI: And our society doesn't provide child care. It doesn't provide for medical or dental care. It just comes right down to the basic level of existence. It burns people out, which means we can't keep doing our work or doing it effectively. But we get strength from seeing the responses, from seeing what it means to people. You see yourself as part of a bigger movement happening in the world, a movement towards justice. It really does feel like that when I remember what we are doing.

AFTERWORD

And in our times
from concepts of empowerment to its negation
a story of women whose backs are broken
who have forgotten to fight
drag existence, drudgery
down on their knees in kitchens
farms
factories
distorted
assaulted

internally collapsed
imbalanced
afraid of their bodies
a story of women in our times

The struggle begins
women's struggle
a struggle for recovery
a search for spine
spine— a metaphor for freedom

Program notes from choreographer Chandralekha

I know no woman— virgin, mother, lesbian, married, celibate—
whether she earns her keep as a housewife, a cocktail waitress, or a
scanner of brain waves— for whom her body is not a fundamental
problem: its clouded meaning, its fertility, its desire, its so-called

frigidity, its bloody speech, its silences, its changes and mutilations, its rapes and ripenings. There is for the first time today a possibility of converting our physicality into both knowledge and power.
Adrienne Rich, Of Woman Born

Finally, whether or not we are dancers, what does it mean to live in this land of our bodies, in its territories of power and powerlessness? In the years of researching and writing this book, I have followed traces of the body mapped through dance, seeing a land of natural power and knowledge in the shifting shapes of women's gestures. The research confirmed my initial impression— that dance can be read as the embodied record of a spiritual and philosophical heritage central to women's culture. The interviews which came late in the project reconfirmed this initial awareness. I was deeply moved by the love and determination of these dancers and by their absolute belief in the body as the source and carrier of spirit and imagination. Hearing their stories, I felt myself returning to a dimly remembered place of trust and confidence in my own body, to the "rightness" that can be felt at the level of the body.

The narrative tendency is to summarize, to draw a conclusion or an end, but the story of women and dance is built around the shifting narrative of the body. Dance is not just about making the body visible— it is about knowing the body in a deeply spiritual, political, and social way. It is about taking risks with the body and constantly challenging this culture's assumptions about the body, and though some dancers would not say so, it is about women's right to define the body on our own terms.

In *The Second Sex*, Simone de Beauvoir cites dancers, actresses, and singers as examples of free women throughout history because, she says, these are women who have earned their own living. This view is full of contradictions, yet it is true that dancers have, as a group, created a historical identity enlivened by the pleasure of working through the body. All of these women have chosen to dedicate their lives to the body, building, as Rina Singha says, a life which would always allow them to say yes to dance, to the body, and to themselves.

I can't help wondering what we, as a culture and a people, would look like if we said yes to the body with the same kind of intensity. What would our world look like if we began from the body? I can't help thinking that our drinking water would still be safe, we would not have a threatening hole in the ozone layer, or pesticides and hormones poisoning our food. As Isadora Duncan recognized so clearly, the body *is* nature, and whatever we have done to nature we have done first to ourselves. Dance alone cannot reverse this callous disregard of nature and our environment, but it can serve to remind us of the fact that whatever else we may be, we are bodies and we are *of* nature, and dance can return us to an original condition of power and knowledge in the body.

Initially, I thought that I could write simply about my own and other people's work in the studio— the reworking of muscles and habits, the stretches for opening up the body, and the re-enactment of women's gestures in dance. But there is another layer I keep returning to that I feel is the real imaginative impulse behind this work, and that is the sense of what it would be like to live first from the body. I have since recognized this as a return to a maternal consciousness deeply embedded in the body.

Before I left for New York, I visited with my mother, who told me a story about our neighbour, a devout Catholic and mother of ten children. This woman had once confided to my mother that she had had ten children, not because she wanted them, but because she was afraid of what our parish priest would say if she didn't regularly produce a child. Our neighbour, along with many of the other women in the rural Catholic community where I was raised, lived out in her daily life the violations of patriarchy brought about by the control of sexuality and motherhood. Even in her most intimate moments, her body was never her own.

Robin Morgan wrote that "Women do not have self-determination over our most basic land... our bodies, which have been regarded as exploitable resources of sex and children." For most women, this describes our experience of the body, whether or not we live it to the extent our neighbour did. By that I mean that we may not all have ten children out of fear, but we have all been educated into the habit of turning away from our body and its desires. This habit has been so deeply absorbed that it is difficult to see "the body as a clear place" (to quote Erick Hawkins) or to believe that any truth about ourselves could ever be brought out of such a conflicted, confused space. Our neighbour lived out an idea of sexuality and motherhood that went against what she knew in her body. This idea distorted her experience of sexuality and motherhood, and it distorted an even more fundamental experience: the power to know and think through the body.

In 1958, the British artist and psycho-analyst Marion Milner wrote a book about keeping a diary. For Milner, this book was part of a larger on-going attempt to trace her creative process as an artist and to understand the truth of her life. Sifting through her days, she surprised herself by finding moments of great clarity in small, seemingly insignificant, events which might easily be passed over: a flock of birds taking flight, the pulse of a jelly-fish in water, the sound of water lapping against a stone.

While reflecting on the significance of these moments, Milner recognizes in these "beads" a kind of inward turning to the body which she then tries to unfold in a more conscious way:

> But once one starts being behind one's eyes, attending to what one's body feels like from inside, especially to the totality of the feeling of its weight, it's then that there is liable to come what I once called the "answering activity," something seems to open up... and one's breathing gets deeper.

In her own private way, Milner works through the equation of women thinking through the body, and at one point in her exploration, she explicitly relates this work to dance, though she is not herself a dancer:

When I considered this bit about the dancing... it certainly seemed to me to do with moving from some other source than one's deliberative mind and finding that the result was not chaos or disaster; an "other" seemed to have taken over and be doing the producing, if only I would trust it and give it a chance.

Milner, like Carrington and H.D., stepped outside the boundaries of reason to find a kind of knowledge she could call her own. In a very real sense, the body is the territory of this knowledge and dance, the map into the territory.

It was never my intent to present a comprehensive history of women in dance. Rather, I have been very selective in my choice of material, choosing examples and stories that illustrate specific ideas about women and the body. Fundamentally, these ideas relate to the construction and transmission of knowledge from the maternal body. The body is the land of our mothers, their place of unreserved knowledge and power, and dance has been the language of this knowledge.

As an undergraduate student I worked with Mary O'Brien, feminist political theorist and author of *The Politics of Reproduction*. Mary maintained that we have no "philosophy of birth" and that we desperately needed a life-centred philosophy to counterbalance the threatening forces of patriarchy with its emphasis on abstraction and death as the true conditions of knowledge. We do have, I think, a philosophy of birth. It is in the gestures of all the dancers whose life works throughout history affirm the truth of the body.

With dance, we have been able to create our own space, an internal space that allows us to know and move from deep within the body, and an external social space that most clearly defines that inner vision. This has been particularly important because of the colonization which has occurred at the level of our bodies. As we have seen, the space where dance exists is not free of conflicts, many of which reflect the conflicts felt by women in everyday life: concern over weight and appearance, conflict between our sexuality and society's regulation of the body, conflict between our need for security and the poverty implied by a career as a dancer. At the same time, dance has been a place of comfort, companionship, and inspiration, a place where women have passed on their knowledge and their art from generation to generation. And a place where we have been able to articulate knowledge and power from the female body.

Continuity is critical to the development of knowledge, if only to let us know what is possible. The history of dance provides a strong, relatively uninterrupted tradition of women artists. In this field, we do not have to begin with the question, "Why have there been no great women artists [dancers]?" which Linda Nochlin asked in relation to women in the visual arts. In fact, the history of dance provides a marked contrast to art history, illustrating a strong tradition of women artists. In her autobiography, American dancer and choreographer Twyla Tharp writes that as an art history student and a fledgling dancer she looked at both traditions and asked herself:

Where were the women? In pre-classic, Greek, Romanesque, medieval, Renaissance, baroque, rococo, and Romantic art, where was one woman's name we all knew? Where in the history of art— music, architecture, painting, sculpture, most centuries of literature— had a woman made a difference? Sometimes I stole time from memorizing the required art history and looked through the meagre dance sections in the stacks. There in the dance collection of the public library, I found my answer: images of Isadora Duncan, Mary Wigman, Doris Humphrey, Ruth St. Denis, and Martha Graham. These women were the pioneers of a new art form. In creating modern dance, they had struck out on their own, and running my fingers over the plates, I literally tried to absorb their power and authority. In their art form, they were genuinely potent— not relegated to second class status, not dilettantes, dabblers, Sunday painters. They could only have done this in America, where women were gaining equality earlier, and this too mattered to me. I was not interested in entering a profession where I was handicapped by second class status. Now I knew both what I was doing in art history and dance, and when graduation day came I skipped the ceremonies. Working toward becoming an artist in a way that I could understand, I chose to go to a rehearsal instead.

Given her tremendous drive and energy, Tharp would have probably become a dancer anyway, but this identification with a community of women did help her take her place as an artist.

Tharp mentions only the presence of women in Western dance, but women all over the world and in different historical periods have always danced and have left behind evidence of their achievements. Not only are these achievements well documented, but we find among them records of dances created by and for women that invoke themes which have emerged elsewhere in women's work: motherhood and women's response to fertility; the association of women and nature; the celebration of goddess figures; and the expression of a body-based spirituality. Gloria Orenstein, in her book on the goddess, writes that the task of feminist writers, artists, and critics is "nothing less than re-membering the body (of culture) of the Great Mother." Women's dances are a literal re-membering of that body and they show us the vast connections women have made in the body.

Maternal, land, knowledge, power— what continuity is there between the words which keep on turning up?

In my first year of study in New York, I remember feeling how working the body was so much like working the farmland I had known as a child. After all those years of trying to leave the farm behind I had actually carried it with me through this commitment to dance and the body. In its origins, so much of dance is this kind of devotion or dedication to the land of the body.

Entry from my journal, November 5, 1984
Some days I hear the land speaking in me as I roll across the

studio floor, feeling my skin stick against the wood. Working the body/working the land: the laboured breath caused by slow, steady plodding to an end, each day working and reworking the same muscles, success and failure one and the same, bound by the necessity of continued work now in the land of the body.

January 22, 1985
The body is a huge piece of work moving silently across the land— itself the unspoken geography...

The body has been interpreted in many different ways— the social body, the moral body, the sexual body, the cultural body. Each of these is a way of listening to and speaking with the body, a way of trying to open the voice of the body and to open to the voice of the body. And yet beneath them all there is another voice breaking through that does not allow interpretation, a voice that is simply the body speaking. I have heard and seen other dancers speak with this internal voice which starts from the body, trusting the lines and sounds that surface from the place of the body.

What do we hear when we think through the body, when we listen quietly to the voice inside the flesh as it speaks in its strange tongue that the tongue in the mouth can't capture? The body as a tongue that says what cannot be said otherwise, the place of subtle and silent speech.

I, like many women, approached dance with questions about my body, about my mother's body, about what history and culture have made of this body of women. Answers came in fragments as I leafed through images of women dancing, as I watched women move on stage, in the studio, or in the street, and as I myself danced or listened quietly to my body. Sometimes the answers came in phrases: "the sagacity of the body," "an informed body," "muscle consciousness," "the grain of a movement." Or in unexpected movements and gestures: the dropping motion of Sun Ock Lee's body in dance meditation, the wild abandon of Pat Hall Smith in performance, Sara Pearson simply and playfully pointing to her hand. These phrases and movements reverberated in my body, like Milner's beads slowly lifting pieces of consciousness from the body's warm response.

> This book is finished, I said. But out of the gap that this word left there grew the certainty that something else must be said. What? About the gap?... What then, the private meaning, private for me?
> *Marion Milner, Eternity's Sunrise*

I began this work wanting to know more about ways of knowing that included women and the body. Throughout the writing of it, I have been accompanied by a stern, internal voice that says that these ways of knowing do not produce the "right" kind of knowledge, that the truth of our bodies cannot be proven outside of our own "subjective responses." And of what value is knowledge without proof? When I listen to this voice, I imagine that I feel as Virginia Woolf did when she thought she had failed to tell the truth of the body.

Like poetry, the truth of the body is intensely personal and intimate, and like poetry, the value of this knowledge has been difficult to place in our "progressive, technological" times.

When I think of all the problems that confront the planet, it almost seems naïve to believe that dance could make a global difference to our well-being. Yet our most serious problems have to do with a disregard of very simple physical needs and with social and productive processes that have intruded on the body to such an extent that we are threatening our own existence.

In her book, *What Is Found There: Notebooks on Poetry and Politics*, Adrienne Rich writes about the revolutionary artist who, without shame, draws on the powers of the natural world, the body, and women, and who "conjures a language that is public, intimate, inviting, terrifying, and beloved." Dance took me into this world of revolutionary artists, and into my own place of revolution. I would say that after all these years, I am still looking to inhabit my body, but I am no longer as guarded or wary and I am more knowing of the pleasure and necessity of this work for us all.